Empath

Healing People with Positive Energy is a Gift.
Master Your Emotions and Set Sensitive
Boundaries to Empower Cognitive, Emotional,
and Compassionate Empathy

By Sharon Copeland

Please consult a licensed professional before attempting any techniques outlined in this book.

Table of Contents

Introduction

An empath enables us to see the user from more points of view. Patterns state a lot, as well as contradictions-- which is essential information. It can occur that a user is not happy about the service but still utilizes it. Alternatively, they have a very positive feeling about service, however not using it as frequently. These are concerns that require to be researched even more.

Although it is a beneficial tool to visually introduce a user, it ought to be taken into account that an empathy map reveals a state at a specific moment in time. For that reason, it is worth returning to your plan from time to time and keep including presumptions and insights, particularly after talking or observing with consumers similar to your profile.

An animal's empath is an empath that is known for its capability to understand animals' mental state and their capacity to connect with their emotions. He very likely might be an animal empath. However, it is tough to state so with any certainty.

But in my own experience, empathy tends to be extremely caring, nurturing, and emotionally available by nature and is generally a donor rather than a taker. What kind of work are empaths doing? The most common service work incorporates their donations to "serve" those who most need them. Most empathies are highly emotional and intuitive, simply because they are more instinctively connected to other people's emotions and needs. Many social scientists describe empathy as having a REAL "6th sense," which is the ability of most of us to identify, understand, and ultimately connect with human beings and their problems.

This leads to an astonishing amount of insight and intuition, which can limit unexplained news. Some recent studies suggest that the sixth sense of emotional empathy is a more developed brain in two specific areas. What are they?

The brain area that modules a sense of "connection" to others and an area deep in the brain that is intended to trigger synesthesia, a little known but proven phenomenon in which people hear colors and hear sounds. (All from the psychic ability to divine contact to seeing auras. This is also seen by many as a potential scientific explanation for everything) What is the "empathy" definition? Does it mean that I am mental? Or does it say that I am incredibly prone to the emotional feelings of others? And how does empathy affect or influence their abilities in the real world?

An empath is someone who has an unusual strong sense of connection, sensitivity, or sympathy to others' emotions and feelings. The word sensible is probably the word that expresses the essence of what empathy IS more effectively than any other term, but this does not imply that they are emotionally sensitive.

Are all empaths mental? Not totally. Not. But inexplicably, many. And by integrating these two little-intended capacities, you get people who are incredibly attuned to others' emotional levels; they can also see future events, so anticipate the consequences where you are now. One of the most forms of psychic ability is psychic empathy. Psychic empathy is people who can feel other people's emotions. A right gift lies in a rare ability to concentrate on people's energies or emotions. They also have the psychological capacity to adapt to spiritual guides. They are essentially messengers. These can offer knowledge from the spiritual realm and help explain one's internal, emotional states.

The more in sync we are with our feelings, the better it is to tap into other people's emotions. Nonetheless, the most common problem is that we are excessively associated with others. Psychic Empaths often fight with it. A lot of self-care is needed for psychic empathy. The gift of psychic empathy can be challenging. They have to defend themselves by setting appropriate limits with their subjects. Take, for instance, the person who recently had a near person's death. The psychic empath experiences the same tiredness, sorrow, and anger as the person who just lost his loved one. The psychic empathy must develop the appropriate ability to protect itself from this. You must learn to separate your own emotions from others'.

Definitions. Subjects. Several techniques can help the psychic empathy to do this. The most popular method is basic meditation. This is a kind of meditation in which empathy connects them to the earth spiritually, emotionally, and visually. It allows them to ground their bodies and mind to the earth's power.

This relationship will hold empathy in its own body and prevent it from getting lost in the emotional realm. Protection meditation is another popular technique. The sensing or visualization of divine protective light is part of a protective meditation. Empaths use this spiritual light as a buffer between its feelings and that of its subjects. While they can still feel others' emotions, they are shielded from "taking up" other people's emotions.

Professional empathy can deliver powerful psychological lectures. You are exceptionally skilled in communicating with guides, angels, or deceased loved ones of your subject. If you have an abundance of negative or overwhelming emotions, psychic empathy can help. We help you discover what affects your feelings and give you the tools you need to deal with them. They can also convey essential messages from the spirit world, often giving you a sense of growing as a person.

In order to maximize the value you receive from this book, O highly encourage you to join our private community on Facebook. Here you will be able to connect and share your thoughts with like-minded people, interested in self-help and healing to continue your journey.

>>Click Here to Join Our Private Support Group<<

You can also get in touch with me at the following contacts:

Website
sharoncopeland.com

Email
info@sharoncopeland.com

Facebook Page
https://swiy.io/SharonCopelandFBPage

Facebook Support Group:
https://swiy.io/SharonCopelandFBGroup

Instagram
@saroncopelandauthor

Get in touch with me for any feedback or question, I can't wait to hear from you soon!

Your Free Gift

You read it right! There is a Second Book waiting for you!

What is the cost? Zero! (0 $/€/£) or any currency you would usually pay with :)

As a way of saying thanks for purchasing my book, I decided to offer you access to a FREE Copy of my book

Self-Help is a way to enhance our own spiritual and physical power. Self-Help is key to living a positive life and goes hand in hand with Empath. I consider it to be a good complimentary reading for empaths who want to take back self-control and more in general want to get a better understanding on some self-help techniques.

SHARON COPELAND

Back to

Self-Help

Self-Healing Tips to Take Care of Your Body and Spirit.
Overcome Stress, Depression, and Panic Attacks with
Mindfulness Meditation

>>Tap Here to Discover the Secrets of effective Self-Help<<

MY OTHER BOOKS

Empath: Healing People with Positive Energy is a Gift. Master Your Emotions and Set Sensitive Boundaries to Empower Cognitive, Emotional, and Compassionate Empathy

MY AUTHOR PAGE

>>Click here to go to my Amazon Author Page for new books<<

And now..Hope you enjoy the gift! Happy reading!

Sharon

Chapter 1

Empathy

Empathy means incorporating a broad series of emotions. This includes looking after other people and having the desire to help them, experiencing emotions that match another person's feelings, discerning what another individual is feeling or belief. It can also be comprehended as having the separateness of specifying oneself and another.

It's also the capability to relate to another individual and feel emotions. Some believe that empathy includes the capability to match another's feelings. In contrast, others think that empathy involves being tenderhearted toward others.

Feeling empathy can include having the understanding that numerous factors go into decision making and cognitive thought processes. Previous experiences have an impact on the decision making these days. Understanding this allows an individual to have compassion for people who frequently make illogical decisions to a problem that many people would react with an obvious response. Damaged homes, childhood injury, lack of parenting, and numerous other aspects can influence the brain's connections, which an individual utilizes to make future decisions.

A psychologist who studied the advancement of empathy said that everybody is born with sensation empathy.

Sympathy and compassion are terms connected with empathy. Meanings differ, adding to the difficulty of specifying empathy. Sympathy is frequently defined as an emotion we feel when others remain in need, encouraging us to help them. Compassion is a sensation of care and understanding for someone in need. Some consist of compassion, a thoughtful issue, and a sensation of the problem for another.

Empathy is also distinct from pity and emotional contagion. Pity is a sensation that one feels towards others that might be in trouble or need aid. As they can not repair their issues themselves, typically referred to as "regretting" for somebody. Psychological contagion is when a person (specifically a baby or a member of a mob) imitatively "catches" the feelings that others are showing without necessarily acknowledging this is happening.

Considering that empathy includes understanding other individuals' emotions, the method they characterize is derived from the method feeling are defined. If, for instance, emotions are taken to be centrally characterized by bodily feelings, then understanding the physical sensations of another will be primary to compassion. If a mix of beliefs and desires more centrally identifies emotions, then grasping these beliefs and desires will be more critical to empathy. The capability to imagine oneself as another individual is a sophisticated creative procedure. The standard capacity to acknowledge emotions is most likely inherent and may be accomplished automatically. Nevertheless, it can be achieved and trained with numerous degrees of strength or accuracy.

Compassion necessarily has a "more or less" quality. The paradigm case of an empathic interaction involves a person communicating an accurate acknowledgment of the significance of another individual's continuous deliberate actions. Associated emotions and personal attributes in a way that the recognized individual can endure. Recognitions that are both tolerable and precise are the main features of compassion.

The human capability to acknowledge physical feelings belongs to one's imitative capabilities. It appears to be grounded in a natural ability to associate the facial expressions and physical motions one sees in another with the proprioceptive sensations of producing those matching expressions. Human beings appear to make the same immediate connection between the intonation and other vocal expressions and inner sensations.

In the field of favorable psychology, empathy has likewise been compared with altruism and egotism. Selflessness are habits that are focused on benefiting another person. At the same time, egotism is a behavior that is acted out for personal gain. Often, when somebody is feeling empathetic towards another individual, acts of altruism take place. Many concern whether or not these acts of selflessness are motivated by egotistical gains. According to favorable psychologists, people can be appropriately moved by their compassion to be altruistic. Others consider the incorrect moral learning perspectives, and having empathy can result in polarization, fire up violence, and encourage dysfunctional behavior in relationships.

Why do we need empathy?

Since it helps us understand how others feel so we can respond appropriately to the situation, empathy is crucial. It is usually connected with social behavior. A lot of research study reveals that the greater empathy one has, the more helpful behavior they possess.

This is not always the case. Empathy can also inhibit social actions and even cause amoral behavior. For instance, someone who sees an automobile accident and is overwhelmed by emotions witnessing the victim in severe discomfort might be less likely to assist that person.

Likewise, intense compassionate sensations for members of our own family or our own social or racial group might lead to hate or hostility towards those we view as a risk. Consider a mother or dad securing their baby or a nationalist protecting their nation.

Some individuals are proficient at checking out others' feelings. Such as manipulators, psychics, or fortune-tellers, may utilize their outstanding, compassionate skills for their benefit by tricking others.

Remarkably, people with higher psychopathic traits. Generally, it shows more utilitarian reactions in moral problems such as the footbridge issue. In this idea experiment, people have to decide whether to press a person off a bridge to stop a train ready to eliminate five others lying on the track.

The psychopath would, more often than not, pick to push the person off the bridge. Following the practical viewpoint of conserving five people's lives by killing one person is a good idea. One might argue that those with psychopathic tendencies are more moral than typical people. Who most likely would not push the individual off the bridge-- as they are less affected by feelings when making moral decisions.

Indications Of Empathy

Some indications reveal that you tend to be an empathetic person:

- You are good at genuinely listening to what others need to state.
- People often tell you about their problems or if they have problems.
- You are very good at picking up on how other people are feeling.
- You frequently think of how other individuals feel.
- Other people come to you for recommendations.
- You often feel overwhelmed by awful occasions.
- You try to help other people who are suffering.
- You are good at informing when individuals are not sincere.
- You sometimes feel drained or overwhelmed in social circumstances.
- You care deeply about other individuals.
- You discover it hard to set borders in your relationships with other individuals.

Having a great deal of empathy makes you worried for the well-being and joy of others. It also indicates, however, that you can, in some cases, get overwhelmed, stressed out, and even overstimulated from always considering other people's emotions.

We frequently find out about the requirement for more empathy on the planet. No doubt you have experienced this in one form or another: The manager who can not connect with his team's struggles, and vice versa-- partners and other halves who no longer understand each other. The moms and dads have forgotten what teenage life resembles, and the teen can not see just how much his daddies and mamas care.

However, if we wish others to consider our viewpoints and feelings, why do we typically stop working to do the same for them?

For one thing, it requires time & effort to understand how and why others feel the way they do. Frankly, we are not willing to invest those resources for too many individuals. Moreover, even when we are encouraged to show empathy, doing so is not simple.

Learn we must; otherwise, our relationships degrade as one individual remains fixated on others' failings. The result is an emotional and psychological standoff where everyone adheres to their guns, no problems get fixed, and situations appear irreconcilable. Nevertheless, making an effort to reveal empathy can break the cycle. Since when an individual feels comprehended, they are most likely to reciprocate the effort and attempt more complicated.

The result? In a relationship where both parties are encouraged to offer the other person the advantage of the doubt and forgive minor failings.

What is empathy exactly? Moreover, how can you establish yours?

What Is Empathy And What It Is Not?

Today, you will get different meanings for empathy, depending on whom you ask. A lot of would concur with some variation of the following. Empathy is the means to share and understand the concepts or sensations of another.

To feel and show empathy, it is not essential to share the same experiences or scenarios. Instead, empathy is an effort to better understand the other person by learning more about their perspective.

Empathy Have Three Classifications

- Cognitive empathy is the ability to explain how a person feels and what they might be believing. Cognitive empathy makes us better communicators since it helps us relay info that best reaches the other individual.
- Emotional empathy (likewise known as affective empathy) is the capability to share another person's sensations. Some have described it as "your discomfort in my heart." This kind of empathy helps you construct emotional connections with others.
- Thoughtful empathy (also called compassionate issue) exceeds just understanding others and sharing their sensations: it moves us to take action, to help nevertheless, we can.

If today we understand compassion as a method of understanding and feeling the emotional lives of others. One hundred years ago, surprisingly, empathy took place with objects of art and nature. Understanding this permits a person to have compassion for individuals who sometimes make illogical decisions to a problem that many people would respond with an apparent reaction. According to favorable psychologists, individuals can be effectively moved by their empathies to be selfless. Others consider the wrong ethical learning point of view and having compassion can lead to polarization, ignite violence, and encourage dysfunctional behavior in relationships.

Taking the effort to reveal empathy can break the cycle-- since when a person feels comprehended, they are more likely to return the effort and effort harder.

Chapter 2

Cognitive Empathy

To begin, think of all the people in your life. Is there someone you turn to when you need a solution to a problem? Somebody who can cut through your emotional mess and assist you in formulating a plan of action?

These go-to problem-solvers typically depend on cognitive empathy to make sense of other individuals' battles. Cognitive empathy is an attribute of emotional intelligence or EQ. It is especially helpful in leadership and the work environment. In this chapter, you will discover what cognitive empathy is and the appropriate methods to use it.

What Is Cognitive Empathy?

Cognitive empathy means you know and comprehend another's problem on an intellectual level without handling their emotions as your own. Cognitive empathy enables you to respond to another individual's emotions in regards to logic more than feelings. It is a type of Emotional Intelligence (EQ), which is the ability to determine and handle one's own emotions, in addition to the feelings of other people.

Emotional intelligence includes three essential abilities:

- We are achieving emotional awareness or the capability to identify and call your own emotions.
- Harnessing those emotions and applying them to jobs like thinking and analytical.
- Managing emotions, which includes both regulating your sensations and helping others to do the same.

A person must have the ability to determine the differing emotions. Handle their feelings and use believing skills to regulate their own and other person's feelings to exercise this empathy type. A legal peacemaker may need to help a married couple sort through their big feelings surrounding a divorce. For many, this would be a mentally taxing experience loaded with stress and harmed sensations. The arbitrator needs to understand the couple's feelings while staying calm and detached themselves. If the mediator were to begin shouting or weeping, the settlements would pertain to a screeching stop.

How To Utilize Cognitive Empathy

As you may have already known, cognitive empathy can be especially helpful in work environment circumstances. Such as settlements, in assisting to inspire others, and understanding others' varied points of view. This kind of compassion is likewise required and used by instructors and teachers routinely.

Leaders and workers who have strong cognitive empathy or high emotional EQ skills can get in another person's head. To comprehend what they desire or what they are trying to interact with. It can be incredibly supportive to understand what another feels and provide merely the correct amount of assistance. This kind of empathy gives clarity and insight to help recenter the person.

Cognitive empathy is essential to lots of work environments. It assists in dealing with conflicts, builds efficient teams, and improves relationships with customers and colleagues. When utilized effectively, cognitive empathy makes the other person feel as though you are raising them out of a predicament and into clarity.

Does Cognitive Empathy Ever Backfire?

Simply put, no. Feeling stoppers can camouflage as cognitive compassion. If somebody takes the psychological detachment to an extreme or is detached from their feelings, the individual may concentrate on discovering a lucrative service instead of a reliable one. In these cases, the emotional detachment can appear callous and block a chance to touch another person in a meaningful way. Cognitive empathy needs to include a dash of compassion to be received well.

Building cognitive empathy.

Structure cognitive empathy is about making educated guesses. We typically misinterpret facial expressions and physical movements; a smile can mean happiness or vitality, but it can signify sadness.

So, before you engage with another individual, consider what you know about them, and be willing to read more. Remember that your analysis of another individual's state of mind, behavior, or belief will be affected by your prior experience and unconscious bias. Your instincts might be wrong. Do not be fast to assume or rush to judgment.

After you engage with others, consider any feedback they offer (composed, spoken, body movement). Doing so will help you better comprehend others and their characters and view your ideas and interaction style.

How to Establish Cognitive Empathy

Cognitive empathy is a vital emotional intelligence skill for leaders and expert success—the same concepts used in all life locations, whether in the house or work.

This is a great way to enhance your cognitive empathy by starting with an awareness exercise. Get a note pad or journal and do the following:

1. OBSERVE your ideas without judgment for one week.

2. CHANGE unfavorable or distressed ideas with encouraging thoughts.

3. RESERVE 15-20 minutes daily to rest your mind and focus inward with self-questioning.

4. SHOW UP the volume of your instinct and listen more carefully.

5. PRACTICE reflective listening with your family and good friends or colleagues.

Chapter 3

Emotional Empathy

When somebody uses the quote above or calls themselves an "empath," they are typically referring to emotional empathy. What is the exact meaning of emotional empathy, and how can you develop it?

Emotional empathy is, as they say, the ability to feel what another person is feeling and to be in their shoes figuratively. A few people can do this naturally and are frequently described as empathic or extremely delicate.

An empath is an individual who experiences others' feelings to a severe and struggles to intellectualize their sensations. A highly sensitive person (HSP) is a person that can feel too much, too intensely. Their nervous system processes details repeatedly that might lead to them being overstimulated by their environment. HSPs and empaths can also soak up the emotions of people who are not revealing them. 15-20% of individuals are considered HSPs or empaths.

The extent to which somebody naturally experiences Emotional Empathy may depend on their mirror neurons. According to the American Psychological Association, mirror nerve cells are "a type of brain cell that reacts equally when we act, and when we witness another person carry out the very same action." Neuroscientist Giacomo Rizzolatti, MD, who initially identified mirror neurons by investigating monkeys, states that these neurons could help discuss how we gain from simulating others and why we can instinctively feel other people's emotions.

If you ever experience slipping and falling on ice, you know how painful and silly the experience can be. You might feel embarrassed or stunned. When you see your friend experience the same thing, you will re-experience those same feelings. That is because, in both circumstances, the same part of your brain has activated. You will instinctively comprehend how your buddy feels because you feel it too.

Close Relationships Require Emotional Empathy.

All close social relationships depend upon emotional empathy. This correlation implies that finding out to utilize emotional empathy efficiently is crucial from home to work and in between.

As a parent, you need to leverage your emotional empathy to relate to your child's stressful day on the playground or your teen overwhelmed with homework. You will need emotional empathy to help them process their experience and accompanying emotions. Alternatively, as a staff member or leader, emotional empathy can help you detect your associates' moods and adjust your behavior appropriately if needed.

People who make use of emotional empathy successfully are frequently natural caregivers and caring parents. They can be cherished managers, online marketers, or HR specialists. They can notice signs of tension in colleagues early and design an option or intervene before an issue outgrows control.

Sometimes, Emotional Empathy Can Be Draining

On the other side, emotional empathy can take a toll on a person's emotional wellness. Social scenarios may be very draining if you experience psychological compassion to an extreme and can not separate your feelings from those around you. You may continuously watch for others' unspoken feelings or habits and invest your mental and emotional energy over-analyzing them.

Emotional empathy is particularly problematic when you focus on another individual's challenges and burdens more than your own. If you are gasping for emotional oxygen, you cannot help or be fully present to someone else. As everybody has heard on airplane flights, "you need to put your oxygen mask on before assisting others." Even though we might tune these words out since we have heard the saying so often, it doesn't make them any less true. In professions like nursing, it is crucial to care for and nurture oneself to maintain emotional and mental health.

Structure Of Emotional Empathy

To accomplish emotional empathy, we need to go one step further. The objective is to share the sensations of the other individual, leading to a much deeper connection.

When an individual tells you about an individual struggle, listen thoroughly. Resist the urge to evaluate the person or situation, interrupt and share your individual experience, or propose an option. Instead, focus on comprehending the how and why: how the person feels and why they feel that way.

Next, it is essential to take some time to show. When you have a much better understanding of how the person feels, you must discover a way to understand.

Ask yourself: When have I felt the same way or similar to what this person has explained?

If a person states, 'I messed up a discussion,' I do not consider a time I screwed up a discussion-- which I have done but then thought. It is no big deal. Rather than, I think of a time I did feel I messed up, possibly on a test or something else crucial to me. It is the sensation of when you failed that you wish to remember, not the event.

You will never have the ability to envision precisely how another person feels. However, attempting will get you a lot closer than you would be otherwise.

Once you discover a method to connect with the other person's feelings and have a complete image of the circumstance, you're ready to reveal caring empathy. In this step, you do something about it to help nevertheless you can.

How to Establish Emotional Empathy

If you have a hard time keeping close emotional relationships, you may need to establish emotional empathy. Luckily, you do not require to be an empath to have psychological compassion. Psychological compassion is an ability that can be discovered.

Put yourself in their position: Before responding, ask yourself, "What would I do if I remained in the other person's scenario? How would I feel?"

Do not react with feeling stoppers. Feeling stoppers prevail in responses to another's emotional crisis to help them feel much better quickly or prevent feeling uneasy. They are the knee-jerk reactions such as coming to the rescue, rejecting that the other person's feeling or issue is genuine, or expressing pity.

Build a compassionate action: The next time a good friend vents to you about a problem, attempt to:

- See the world as they see it.
- Dedicate to being nonjudgmental.
- Attempt to comprehend the other person's feelings.
- Interact your understanding of those sensations.
- If you do not understand, get curious.

Emotional Empathy Can Be Both Excellent and Bad.

Because it means that we can readily understand and feel other people's emotions, emotional empathy is good. This is crucial for those in caring professions. Such as nurses and doctors, to be able to react to their clients appropriately. When they are distressed, it also means that we can respond to friends and others.

Emotional empathy is terrible because it is possible to end up being overwhelmed by those feelings. For that reason, they are not able to respond. This is known as empathy overload. Those with a tendency to end up being overwhelmed with emotional empathy need to work on their self-regulation, particularly their self-control, to manage their feelings.

Good self-discipline helps medical professionals and nurses to prevent possible burnout from empathizing excessively. However, there is a threat that they can end up being 'solidified' and not respond appropriately. There have been several current cases in the UK, such as in South Staffordshire, where others and nurses were unconcerned. This may have been a possible outcome of over-protection against empathy overload.

Chapter 4

Compassionate Empathy

The expression "decide with your head, not with your heart" would make you believe that emotional empathy and cognitive empathy can not coexist. This is not true when the heart and mind meet in the middle; the 3rd type of empathy comes alive-- Compassionate Empathy.

Deep empathy is the antithesis of knee-jerk reactions. It is often the ideal reaction to challenging circumstances as this ability blends intelligence, emotion, and action by thinking about the whole person. By establishing compassionate empathy, you will go beyond a basic understanding of interactions, whether emotional or intellectual. You will have the ability to nurture a much deeper connection with others and feel comfortable no matter what another individual is sharing with you.

What Is Compassionate Empathy?

Compassionate empathy is the ability to share and comprehend another individual's feelings without taking them on as your own emotions or blurring the line between you and another individual. It uses emotional intelligence to adequately react to a circumstance without being overwhelmed or attempting to repair anything. It empowers the other individual to step into their power.

Whereas cognitive empathy might be the very best action in intellectual disputes, emotional empathy may move into equipment when it pertains to our loved ones. Compassionate empathy is what we think about to be a typical response to many scenarios. That is because it considers the whole individual.

When we state that compassionate empathy "thinks about the entire individual," we imply that it:

- Seeks to connect with the other person, see the world through their eyes, and comprehend their feelings without an overlay of your feelings.
- Focuses on the other person with a gentle interest and without being connected to a specific outcome.
- Compassionately acknowledges and confirms feelings without encouraging, unless asked for.
- Creates a safe area for the other individual to share and fix their struggle.
- It helps manage the other individual's feelings and ground them into their inner strength and wisdom.
- Links the individual to their own heart and reasoning, which increases insight, significance, and the courage to act.

Compassionate vs. Cognitive vs. Emotional Empathy

Let us examine a scenario and the difference between actions built upon thoughtful empathy versus responses fixated by emotional or cognitive empathy.

Situation:

Your friend at work, looking distraught, concerns your desk and says, "Mitch disrupted my discussion, and in front of the director! I do not understand what I'm going to do; I'm so furious. He constantly believes he knows much better. I simply don't see a way out-- he micromanages everything!"

The Emotional Empathy Action:

You instantly feel the effect of your good friend's emotions. Your heart feels deeply for her scenario-- you've existed. You take your friend's hand, saying, "You have got a right to be angry; that's embarrassing and so disempowering!"

The Cognitive Empathy Action:

You pull up a chair for your buddy and say, "Walk me through what took place. That may shine a light on how we can continue, and I will help you resolve this."

The Compassionate Empathy Response:

You ask your friend to accompany you on a walk outside. When far from the office, you say, "I know how important that presentation was to you; you use a lot of effort into it. That's got to be so shocking! Furthermore, it seems like you are completely fed up with your supervisor." After your good friend's feelings settle, you state, "Inform me more about what occurred and how you plan to handle it."

All three actions promote a connection with the other person and help them return to peacefulness and to discover an option. The compassionate, empathetic response uses all three aspects of empathy while acknowledging the person's whole experience. It helps provide a safe space for the other individual to express themselves, feel heard, and regain their solid ground.

Why Select Compassionate Empathy?

Compassionate empathy is called the middle ground that honors the natural connection between the brain and the heart. As an outcome, there are a few disadvantages to sensation and revealing thoughtful empathy for others! This type of empathy exceeds simply comprehending others and sharing their sensations. It moves us to act; to help at any place we can. It offers the groundwork for sharing experiences AND assists the other individual in growing.

Exercising Compassionate Empathy

You begin by asking the other person directly what you can do to help if they are unwilling or unable to share.

Ask yourself:

What helped me when I failed? Or what would have helped me in this circumstance?

It is fine to tell your experience or even make suggestions. But avoid sending the impression that you have seen it all or have all the answers. Instead, relay it as something that has helped you in the past. Present it as a choice that can be adapted to their circumstances, instead of insisting that it is an all-inclusive answer.

Be aware that what worked for you, or even for others, might not even work for this person. Do not let that restrain you from continuing to assisting other individuals. Just do what you can do.

Putting It Into Practice

Next time when you are having difficulty in seeing someone else's point of view. Remember to strive and apply the following:

- You do not have the whole picture. A person is dealing with too many factors at any given time, most of which you are unaware of.
- The way you feel and think about a situation may be different from each day to the next. You might be influenced by various elements, including your current mood.
- You may behave very differently under emotional stress than you think you would be given to normal circumstances.
- Keeping these in mind will affect how you view someone and influence the way you cope with them. And since every person goes through our struggle at some point or perhaps another, eventually, you will need that same level of understanding.

A person must be able to identify various emotions. Control their emotions and apply thinking skills to modulate their own and others' feelings to exercise this empathy type. On the other hand, psychological empathy can take a toll on an individual's emotional well-being. Emotional compassion becomes particularly problematic when you concentrate on another person's burdens and obstacles more than your own. The adage, "Think with your head, and not with your heart," would make you think that emotional empathy and cognitive empathy can not coexist. When the heart and mind meet in the middle, the third type of empathy comes alive— compassionate empathy.

Chapter 5

Cognitive vs. Emotional Empathy

Can you recall the last time you were with a loved one who was feeling unfortunate or hopeless? Perhaps after a divorce, after they received a life-altering medical diagnosis, or after the loss of a close loved one. Their tears developed a response with us. We felt relocated to wish to comfort them in some way.

We generally think about empathy as the capability to place ourselves in another person's shoes. Did you know that scientists have identified various types of empathy? Two primary kinds of empathy are cognitive empathy and emotional empathy. Although they are somewhat distinct, both are equally crucial for assisting us in forming and maintaining connections with others.

Empathy helps connect people, moving them towards each other in an assisting or healing capability. When you reveal deep empathy toward others, their defense energy decreases, and favorable energy replaces it. When you can get more imaginative in solving problems, that is.

As we live at our work and in the house, we continually balance and interact with relationship dynamics. When we do not have empathy, we cannot establish and nurture those interpersonal connections, resulting in strained relationships, loss of relationships, seclusion, and broken trust.

It ends up being harder to repair conflicts, work collaboratively, or resolve problems when we do not practice empathy.

Our society relies on empathy to help with connections and forward motion. When the empathy piece is missing out on, we become more detached and less efficient in our products and innovative ideas. Practicing empathy is necessary for a variety of relationship dynamics, such as those amongst:

- Service partners.
- Associates.
- Community groups.
- Co-workers.
- Dating Relationships.
- Families.
- Buddies.
- Marital relationships.
- Brother or sisters.

Two different types of empathy expose how we can relate to a pal or member of the family in crisis. There are distinct distinctions between the two types of empathy.

Cognitive Empathy

When we exercise cognitive empathy, we are practicing taking the point of view of another individual. In an aspect, we imagine what it might be like to be this person in their situation. Cognitive empathy is likewise described as perspective-taking. It provides itself to the idea of putting yourself in somebody else's shoes.

With cognitive empathy, you are attempting to take advantage of the concept of positioning yourself in another person's situation and getting a much better understanding of their experience.

When someone we appreciate is harming, it can be easy for us to maintain a range from it since we can see the big picture. For example, if a pal does not get a job she interviewed for, you can more than likely see her disappointment. Nevertheless, you might also recognize that she is talented and will probably find an excellent job soon.

On the other hand, when we practice cognitive empathy, we can satisfy individuals and comprehend why they feel sad or dissatisfied after not getting the job. We practice envisioning what it might be like to be them at that moment, looking at the circumstance or situation from their viewpoints.

In summation:

- Taking another individual's point of view.
- Envisioning what it resembles in another person's shoes.
- Understanding someone's sensations.

Emotional Empathy.

Picture yourself sitting close to a loved one, such as your child, sibling, or close friend, as he or she begins to weep. What he is experiencing is likely having an impact on us, doesn't it? We may start to feel sad too. When we undergo emotional empathy, we are moving from the cognitive perspective-taking into a shared personal experience.

Social psychology scientists Hodges and Myers describe emotional empathy in three parts:

- Experiencing the same feeling as the other individual.
- Feeling our distress in reaction to their discomfort.
- Feeling compassion toward the other individual.

They keep in mind that there is a positive correlation between emotional empathy and the willingness you want to help other people. It is more likely that somebody who finds it easy to practice emotional empathy will be transferred to help that person in need too. It might be easy to see the advantage of emotional empathy in our essential relationships' general health and enjoyment.

In summation:

- Sharing an emotional experience.
- Feeling distressed in response to somebody's pain.
- Experiencing a desire to help somebody.

Other Kinds of Empathy

In addition to emotional and cognitive empathy, a person may experience:

- Affective empathy: This involves the ability to comprehend another person's feelings and respond appropriately.
- Somatic empathy: Having a physical reaction to what another person is experiencing is another method to show empathy. If someone is feeling very embarrassed, you may also blush or have an uneasy stomach.

Nature vs. Nurture

Even though genes have been discovered to influence our capacity to feel empathy, there is much to say about our knowing social experiences. You may have currently heard the phrase "nature vs. support." This expression referrals a long-standing argument amongst researchers, arguing what they think to have a more significant impact on our behaviors, conditions, and traits.

Some scientists suggest that genes are the primary influence, while others believe that our environment and social interactions can help us develop empathy.

Social Knowing

The social knowing theory, established by psychologist Albert Bandura, integrates cognitive wise theory, and behavioral smart theory components.

It is recommended that people can increase their capacity for empathy through modeling and experiencing empathy from others.

When a child has not had anybody to provide their emotional experiences any value, time, or attention, it is understandable how the child might likely continue to experience the world and relationships without this crucial skill of knowing how to feel sorry for others. Here are some examples of the things the child would miss out on.

- Being able to watch and observe someone practicing empathy to understand what it appears like.
- When they are in need, experiencing someone empathizes with them.
- Having somebody teach them the value of emotions.
- Knowing how to construct significant connections with people.

Having empathy helps close an emotional gap between individuals, developing a shared experience and a connection. When we do not know what a shared personal experience seems like with someone, it can be hard to know how to do that with others.

The failure to understand can lead to difficulty at work, in relationships, within families, and within society.

Discovering Balance.

Cognitive and emotional empathy are terrific partners and can be an excellent pair when practiced with balance. The capability to take someone's perspective and understand what it might be like to be them. Meeting somebody emotionally and having a shared emotional experience can be a game-changer for many relationship dynamics.

When people feel seen, heard, and understood, we can do fantastic things together utilizing both emotional and cognitive empathy. This empathetic balance helps enable things like:

- Cooperation.
- Creativity.
- Emotional connection.
- Assessment.
- Feeling safe.
- Recognizing needs.
- Satisfying requirements.
- Settlement.
- Problem-solving.
- Trust.

Excessive Empathy

As valuable and beneficial as the skill of empathy is, it is suggested that too much empathy can be harmful to one's emotional wellness, health, and relationships. Emotional empathy is a foundation of connection between individuals. The subjective experience we shared prompts us to move closer to someone, comfort them, and use reassurance and aid.

However, emotional empathy indicates that our bodies react to our feelings while others' existence and personal experience.

When there is a well-balanced practice of emotional empathy, we can enable the area to share a personal experience with another individual while not letting our emotional reactions get in the way. When our emphatic emotional arousal becomes too high, it can obstruct people from being thoughtful and empathizing.

Feeling mentally dysregulated can end up being frustrating and lead to feeling burned out. Ultimately, this will leave you not wanting to practice empathy because it is too unbearable to be there for someone else.

Our capability to practice emotional empathy ends up being a danger to our well-being when it leads to sensations of seclusion, being misinterpreted, and sensation inauthentic.

Inadequate Empathy

Some people are better at practicing cognitive empathy yet have a challenging time tapping into emotional empathy. These two types of empathy are functioning from entirely various systems of processing. This is the difference between perspective-taking and cognitive processing compared to emotional processing.

When there is an imbalance of empathy-- leaning too heavily on cognitive empathy and inadequate emotional empathy-- our connections with individuals might feel strained. The person you are trying to give your help or comfort may sense that you understand their situation, which can undoubtedly help. It may leave them with the thought that they are a bit misunderstood, unheard, or unseen.

When you practice too much cognitive empathy and not enough emotional empathy, the vital part of having a relative emotional experience with that person at the moment is missing. The following is an easy example of what this may appear like:

Example 1: Cognitive Empathy.

Loved one: My grandmother simply died, and we were close. (Begins to cry.).

A person utilizing cognitive empathy: I'm sorry. I know you are sad. What you are going through is hard.

Example 2: Emotional Empathy.

Loved one: My grandma simply died, and we were genuinely close. (Starts to cry.).

Individual utilizing emotional empathy: I'm sorry to find out about your grandmother. I understand you miss her. I'm here for you. (May end up being tearful or reveal sadness.).

These very simplified illustrations. We can feel what it may feel like for the other individual if we stopped with cognitive empathy and did not bring emotional empathy to the interaction.

The person gets the condolences for her granny doing and knows you are trying to offer comfort. However, there is no opportunity for the individual to have a shared emotional experience with you. The shared emotional experience can feel rather soothing and recovery to somebody in need.

Chapter 6

What is an Empath?

Empaths are susceptible individuals who have an eager capability to notice individuals around them who feel and think.

Psychologists may utilize the term empath to explain a person who experiences great empathy, often to the point of taking on others' discomfort at their own expense. However, the term "empath" can also be a spiritual term describing a specific person with unique psychic abilities to pick up others' emotions and energies. This chapter will concentrate on the psychological aspects of being an empath.

There are lots of benefits to being an empath. On the brilliant side, empaths tend to be excellent good friends. They are outstanding listeners. They consistently show up for buddies in times of need. They are generous and big-hearted. Empaths likewise tend to be mentally smart and highly user-friendly.

Some of the extreme qualities that make empaths such fantastic good friends can be difficult on the empaths themselves. Since empaths feel what their good friends are going through, they can be overwhelmed by painful emotions, such as anxiety or anger. Empaths tend to handle the issues of others as their own. It is usually difficult for them to set boundaries independently and say no, even when asked of too much.

Besides, it is common for empaths to feel drained after hanging around people. Empaths are typically introverts, and they need a specific quantity of alone time to recharge. A research study from 2011 suggests a link between highly empathic individuals and social stress and anxiety. Crowds can feel incredibly overwhelming to empathize, who are typically too conscious of individual sounds and constant chatter. They usually feel their best when they are surrounded by nature.

How do you know if you're an empath?

Empaths are extremely sensitive, carefully tuned instruments when it comes to feelings. They feel whatever, sometimes to an extreme, and are less apt to intellectualize sensations. Instinct is the filter through which they experience the world. Empaths are naturally providing, spiritually attuned, and good listeners. If you want a heart, empaths have got it. Through thick and thin, they are there for you, world-class nurturers.

The trademark of empaths is that they understand where you're coming from. Some can do this without handling people's sensations. However, like myself and many of my clients, others can end up being angst-sucking sponges for much better or worse. This frequently overrides the superb capability to absorb favorable feelings and all that is beautiful. Their bodies take in these and grow if empaths are around peace and love. Negativity, though, often feels assaultive, stressful. Thus, they're especially easy marks for emotional vampires, whose worry or rage can damage empaths. As a subliminal defense, they may gain weight as a buffer. When thin, they are more vulnerable to negativeness. A missing out on the reason for overindulging. Plus, an empath's level of sensitivity can be frustrating in romantic relationships. Numerous remain single, considering that they have not found out to negotiate their unique cohabitation requires a partner.

When empaths soak up the impact of stressful emotions, it can activate anxiety attack, depression, drug, food, and sex binges, and a myriad of physical signs that defy traditional medical diagnosis from tiredness to agoraphobia. Because I am an empath, I want to help all my empath-patients cultivate this capacity and be comfortable.

Empathy doesn't need to make you feel excessive all the time. Now that I can axis myself and refrain from taking on civilization's discontents, empathy continues to make me freer, sparking my compassion, vitality, and sense of the miraculous. To identify whether you're an emotional empath, take the following quiz.

You Can Ask yourself:

- Have I been described as "too emotional" or overly sensitive?
- If a friend is troubled, do I begin feeling it too?
- Are my sensations easily bruised?
- Am I emotionally depleted by crowds, requiring time alone to restore?
- Do my nerves get rattled by sound, smells, or extreme talk?
- Do I choose to take my car to locations so that I can leave when I please?
- Do I overeat to handle emotional stress?
- Am I scared of ending up being swallowed up by intimate relationships?

If your answer is "yes" to 1-3 of these questions, you're at least part empath. Reacting "yes" to more than three indicates that you have found your emotional type.

Acknowledging that you are an empath is the first step in taking charge of your emotions instead of continuously drowning in them. Remaining on top of empathy will enhance your self-care and relationships.

Signs That You Are An Empath

If you are fascinated to find out what exactly defines an empath and have natural emphatic abilities, here are some qualities and signs that you may empathize with you.

Your empathy is inherent.

It is the skill that makes you understand others' experiences and emotions beyond your point of view.

Say your buddy just lost their canine of 15 years. Empathy is what permits you to understand the level of pain she's going through, even if you have never lost a precious animal.

But as an empath, you take things an action even more. You pick up and feel feelings as if they belong to your own experience. Somebody else's discomfort or joy becomes your discomfort or happiness.

Intimacy overwhelms.

Empaths frequently find frequent close contact hard, which can make romantic relationships challenging.

You wish to connect and develop a lasting collaboration. However, spending excessive time with someone results in stress, overwhelm, or stress over losing yourself in the relationship.

You might likewise discover sensory overload or a "torn nerves" feeling from excessive talking or touching. When you try to reveal your requirement for time alone, you absorb your partner's hurt feelings and feel even more distressed.

Setting healthy, clear boundaries can help minimize distress for the empath. Safeguarding your mental and emotional health should also be vital to you; otherwise, energy will be drained from you.

You have the right instinct.

Ever felt like you have a strong inclination to things are not correct? Or maybe you can sense that someone cheated or something is good or bad instinctively? Your empathy is present in this situation.

Empaths tend to detect subtle insights on others' ideas, like telling if a person is truthful or not.

As an empath, you might put a great deal of faith in your instincts when making decisions. While others may consider you spontaneous, the truth is that you are only trusting your intuition to guide you to the right choice for you.

You enjoy nature.

Anybody can gain from spending time in a natural environment. Empaths might feel even more drawn to nature, and remote locations since natural areas offer a soothing space to rest from overwhelming feelings, sounds, and emotions.

You might feel totally at peace when hiking alone in a sunlit forest or viewing waves crash versus the shore. Even a peaceful walk through a garden or an hour sitting under trees might lift your spirits, relieve overstimulation, and aid you to unwind.

You don't thrive in crowded spaces.

According to researchers, empaths can soak up unfavorable or favorable energy by merely being in someone's company. In crowded or busy places, this sensitivity might appear magnified to the point of being almost intolerable.

Empaths feel everything more intensely as compared to an ordinary person. If you can quickly sense how others feel, you'll likely have a tough time handling the emotional "sound" from a crowd, or perhaps a smaller sized group of people, for an extended amount of time.

When you're picking up on negative feelings, energy, or even physical distress from people around you, you may become overloaded or physically unwell. As a result, you may tend to become solitary or limit the company to a few.

You can NOT care.

An empath does not just feel for somebody-- they feel with somebody. Taking in others' feelings so profoundly can make you want to do something about them. Empaths feel obligated to help in any way. In situations where an empath is not able to aid the other person, he feels dissatisfied.

Empaths find it hard to have fun when someone is in pain or is struggling; thus, he will act upon his natural inclination to assist in alleviating their distress, even if that implies absorbing it himself.

Being concerned for others' welfare is not bad, but it may sometimes lead to ignoring your own needs. Overly caring for others can lead to fatigue and burnout, so it's important to conserve some energy.

People easily confide in you.

Sensitive, compassionate individuals tend to be great sounding boards. Other people, especially your loved ones, may feel comforted by your assistance and connect to you first whenever they experience difficulties or troubles.

Because of too much caring for others, empaths have difficulty distinguishing that they are nearly overwhelmed. Therefore, finding a balance is essential. Without limits, unattended generosity and level of sensitivity can pave the way for "emotion dumps" that may be excessive for you to manage at an instant.

Because of their trusting nature, empaths are prone to ploys, abuse, or manipulations. Your earnest desire to assist individuals in distress can leave you unaware of indications of malice or evil.

Since you can sense pain, you better understand the discomfort due to habits and wish to assist. Nevertheless, it is not always up to you if the other person is not ready for your assistance.

You have increased sensitivity to noises, smells, or feelings.

An empath's oversensitivity does not just associate with his emotions. It is not very easy to distinguish between empaths and overly sensitive people, but you may discover that the empath is more sensitive to the world around you.

The signs may include:

- Odors and fragrances affect you more highly.

- Jarring sounds and physical sensations may affect you more strongly.
- You choose to listen to media at low volumes or get information by reading.
- Specific sounds may trigger an emotional response.

You require time to recharge.

Oversensitive persons are easily drained and get fatigued from their exposure to another person's pains and struggles. Even an overload of positive sensations might tire you, so it is essential to put in the time you require to reset.

If you do not shield yourself from negativity, you will likely get burnt out, which may significantly impact your life and health.

Requiring time alone doesn't always imply you're an introvert. Empaths can likewise be extroverts or fall anywhere on the spectrum. Perhaps individuals energize you-- till you reach that point of overwhelming.

Extroverted empaths may require extra care to strike the ideal balance between hanging out with others and restoring their emotional reserves.

You dislike conflict.

You likely dread or actively avoid dispute if you're an empath.

Non-caring people easily hurt oversensitive persons. The slightest criticism, whether intentional or unintentional, will cut into an empath's heart.

Battles and arguments can likewise cause more distress, given that you're not just handling your sensations and reactions. You're also absorbing the feelings of the others included. However, when you wish to attend to everybody's hurt, do not understand how even minor disagreements can end up being harder to manage.

You always feel like the odd man out.

Despite being highly attuned to others' sensations, lots of empaths find it challenging to associate with others.

Others may not understand why you become exhausted and worried so rapidly. You might have difficulty understanding the feelings and emotions you feel or absorb like you are always different from others, leading to the empath keeping to himself. You might avoid speaking about your sensitivities and sharing your intuitions, so you feel less out of place.

The world should understand that it is never easy to feel that you do not belong, yet you care deeply for others. The empath is a special gift to the world. It is uncommon, yes, but it is an essential part of your personality.

You tend to be alone.

Isolation is an empath's sanctuary to allow him to recuperate from the confusing and painful feelings. But taking time out too long can also be damaging to an empath's psychological health. There are various kinds of isolation, and some might provide more therapeutic benefits than others.

Attempt to take your time alone outdoors when possible, practice meditation in a quiet park, walk in the rain, take a picturesque drive, or garden.

Think about adding an animal to your life if individuals drain you quickly. Empaths might connect to animals more extremely and draw deep comfort from this bond.

You find it challenging to set borders.

Boundaries are significant in all relationships.

If you're an empath, you might struggle to turn off the capability to feel and find it difficult to stop giving, even when you have no energy left. When the exact opposite is real, you may believe boundaries suggest you do not care about your loved ones.

Borders end up being even more necessary because others' experiences have such a substantial impact on empaths. They help you set limitations around words or actions that might adversely impact you, allowing you to satisfy your needs.

When you start not to decipher your feelings from others, it might be time to explore a healthy boundary setting with a therapist.

You view things differently.

Your emotions and intuition powerfully drive you, and you are more likely to pick up on things about other people or relate to them on a level that other people cannot.

However, such a connection to others can have its downside. Cultures that suppress free emotional communication can curtail imagination and productivity, leaving the empath to be disengaged, detached, and immature.

You sometimes find it difficult to manage emotional and

sensory overload.

Empaths may often find it challenging to shield their emotions.

Excellent healthy boundaries and self-care practices can assist insulate you, especially from negative emotions and energy. The emotional "sound" of the world can cause significant distress when you lack the tools to handle it.

Suppose you have a hard time managing overstimulation on your own, impacting your lifestyle, or keeping you from relationships and other personal goals. In that case, a therapist can help you learn to develop boundaries and identify useful self-care methods.

Remember, your feelings and needs are just as important as those you pick up in everyone around you.

How is your reading going?

Hi there!

I hope you are enjoying the reading, do you find the information useful?

I've put all my experience and research into the book, I hope you are liking the book!

If you find the information are valuable and interesting, I'd like to kindly ask for your support with leaving a review on Amazon. It would only take 30 seconds of your time but it would make a huge difference to me, and it would help other people like you finding some valuable insights on the topic they are interested in.

>>You can Leave a Review Here<<

Or Scan This Code With your Phone Camera

If you have any feedback, please get in touch with me at the following contacts, I have them at the beginning of the book, but for your convenience I drop them here too!

Website: sharoncopeland.com

Email: info@sharoncopeland.com

Facebook Page: https://swiy.io/SharonCopelandFBPage

Facebook Support Book:
https://swiy.io/SharonCopelandFBGroup

Instagram: @saroncopelandauthor

Happy Reading!

Chapter 7

Kinds of Empath

A great deal of times, an individual immediately connects with people. If loved ones are in trouble, empaths start feeling their emotions. Occasionally, they also try to enter into somebody else's shoes. Do you know why? Because they experience empathy. Though empaths aren't dominating, they can heal and guide. Empaths understand the lives of the people close to them. Deals with their mood swings with a joyful face. Now that we understand the signs of being empathetic let's find out the types of empaths.

1. Claircognizant Empath

The claircognizant empathic trait is derived from both clairaudient, meaning clear hearing, prophecy, and clear seeing or somebody who is perceived as clear understanding. These souls can understand certain things simply, and they are continually being informed with understanding. Vibrant concepts that puzzle and motivate others.

2. Emotional Empath

An emotional empath is an empath that is extremely sensitive to the feelings of other humans. These empaths can get in touch with what others are going through even before they open up.

3. Physical Empath

A physical empath is an empath that is often described as extremely conscious of other human beings' physical suffering. These empaths are incredibly responsive to injured souls. They are known to quite actually feel and physically handle the pain others are going through. Because of that, physical empaths are frequently tired and burnt out. They may even go through life, sensation hostile, or utilized. They have no control over how somebody's tension, discomfort, and emotional output makes their body feel.

4. Fauna Empath or Animal Empath

Fauna empath is known to comprehend the frame of mind of animals and their capability to connect with their emotions. Fauna empaths have potent relationships with animals and are linked with their energies. These empaths are understood to like animals more than human beings and typically express the deeply connected feeling to all types.

An animal empath is thought about as a person with an exceptional capability of acknowledgment. It comprehends an animal's emotions and mindset to such a degree regarding being able to affect its behavior in a favorable method.

Animal empaths have been around throughout history. Very often, this ability was seen as surprising. Francis of Assisi and his capability to "talk" to the animals are the most well-known example.

In the middle ages, animals and males were viewed differently today. Being very "close" to nature is not viewed positively and might even lead to being accused of heresy if your views of nature or animals remained in conflict with church doctrine. Or of demonic possession and even witchcraft if you were seen to be interacting with animals.

When it comes to Francis of Assisi, his credibility for saintliness undoubtedly resulted in his unparalleled capability to indicate his holiness rather than evidence of witchcraft or other evil.

How precisely he could interact with animals, assuming it was not miraculous, is naturally unknown. Evaluating his life story, he was both an intelligent individual, having prospered previously as a merchant, and a compassionate person. He likewise lived a life of austerity and, typically, seclusion.

Surviving on his own and far from his fellow men for extended periods would have meant loneliness. People are not singular beings. Did this solitude in nature, linked with intelligence and potentially an asking mind lead him to observe and find out animal behavior? Was he able to engage with these animals and construct a mutual understanding and trust based on empathy?

There is no other way to know, but we can look at whether any people today genuinely are animal empaths. An animal empath is a person with an exceptional ability to acknowledge and understand the emotions and mindset. Such a degree regarding having the ability to interact with the animal genially affects its behavior in a favorable method.

Residing on his own and far from his fellow guys for extended periods would have indicated loneliness. Human beings are not singular animals. Did this privacy in nature, integrated with intelligence and possibly an asking mind, lead him to observe and find out animal behavior? Was he able to communicate with these animals and develop a good trust and understanding bond based on empathy?

There is no way to know, but we can look at whether any people today genuinely are animal empaths.

There is a well-known National forest hunt at the Matobo Hills National Park in Zimbabwe. It has been interacting with small lizards for years. He learned this ability from his daddy. He will call them, feed them from his hand, and he can hold them. No one else can ever do this, even if they offer the lizard food.

The lizards have discovered that the scout can feed them and that they can trust him. They do not trust anyone else. So is he an animal empath?

I do not think so. What he does is impressive. I do not see him as an animal empath. He utilizes a whistle to "call" the lizards. This call works just like Pavlov's bell. The lizards have found out to associate food with this noise and this noise with the video game scout. They do not trust anybody, not making this sound. This is a trained behavior due to identifying their feelings and mental state and has nothing to do with communicating with the animals.

People with the most significant understanding of animal feelings and have a reasonable frame of mind. Most notably will likely know how animals express themselves and know naturally how animals behave.

Their understanding of animal behavior typically permits them to analyze and comprehend the emotions of animals appropriately.

Frequently this connection develops into an intuition. Such is the circumstance of ethologist and lion specialist Kevin Richards. His fantastic ability with lions is exceptional. His knowledge of lions, their behavior, and the intuition he has developed over several years of engaging with his lions permit him actually to play and go near them. Does this, therefore, mean that he is an animal empath?

Maybe. He is likely a lion empath for sure. However, it is necessary to keep in mind that the lions he interacts with are not wild. Therefore much of their behavior is habituation. So, he most likely could be an animal empath; however, it is hard to say so with any certainty unless we see him connect with wild animals. Seeing the animals he interacts with are lions, I genuinely hope that he does not begin doing the same with wild lions. That might get unpleasant if his capabilities as a lion/animal empath are not particular!

So, do real animal empaths exist? To be more precise, are there any people who can engage and understand wild animals in their natural environment. Without having been uncommonly conditioned or habituated to man?

I have seen some extraordinary unlikely interactions between wild animals and people during the time I invested in wildlife areas.

A number of these interactions are quite typical. It is quite typical for a Zimbabwean Specialist guide to technique elephants on foot and interacts with them. After years of studying and observing elephants in their natural habitat and having been intensively trained to safely approach them, this is not unexpected. You simply get utilized to recognizing their state of mind and how they feel about you and what you are doing.

I expect many people who could be called animal empaths. A couple of actually have a genius for understanding and communicating with animals. Much may be gained from books or experience. However, these couple of extraordinary individuals have a tremendous and innate instinct that sets them apart.

Everyone can study animal behavior and learn how to acknowledge domesticated and wild animals' mental and emotional states. Anyone who deals with animals and their pets should do the same thing if they want to know them better.

Animal empaths are real, and it is not telepathy or magical spiritual connection. It is just understanding, knowledge, and experience. Everyone can end up being an animal empath in some way. However, some people can "talk" to animals.

5. Geomantic Empath

A geomantic empath is somebody who is known to have a deep link with their environments. Geomantic empaths can feel the soul or presence of a specific location, and therefore, they are unconsciously drawn to these destinations. An empath with geomantic tendencies can feel the joy, or the sadness, that a location holds and typically get in touch with older places like graveyards and churches.

6. Medium Empath

A medium empath is an empath that has established a deep and rooted connection with a supernatural force or the deceased. Not only do these empaths get in touch with forces, but they also might not have the ability to see. However, they feel and hear the emotional output of the spiritual world.

A Medium utilizes her senses and sensitivities to explore three-dimensional truth, which permits her to source details from someone's past, present, or future. Mediums can sense energetic types, feelings, and images linked to a person. This can help them address important questions about health, love, relationships, work, and more.

7. Psychometric Empath

A psychometric empath is a very cool ability. It is an empath that can get memories, energy, and detailed information from physical objects. They can collect this information, or these sensations, from fashion jewelry, photos, clothing, etc.

8. Precognitive Empath

A precognitive empath is the sort of empath that has an extremely strong sense of instinct. These individuals will have visions about events that have yet to take place. Precognition provides these empaths with the capacity to predict future incidents, and these visions frequently come to them in their dreams. It is very substantial to keep in mind that in some cases, precognitive empaths do not dream about direct situations that will happen; however, they often dream of signs and symbols that are relevant to the future.

9. Telepathic Empath

A telepathic empath is an ability that can analyze and read someone's inner thoughts. It is thought that each of us has within us the capacity for telepathy; however, not all of us know how to establish it or control it at will. Most people know about a tale of a telephone call got precise at the moment they were thinking about that specific person; maybe instead some-one from way back, who had been on their mind on and off for days, suddenly sounds them out of the blue or appears at a celebration or in the street. Likewise, each of us has probably had the experience where we just know someone is staring at us even though our back is to them; on turning, we find we are area on. Alternatively, we might have stared at some-one, preparing them to look up, which they do seconds later, satisfying our eyes directly even though we may remain in a congested location.

Different Kinds of Telepathy

Two unique kinds of telepathy take the kind of passive and active. Each of us is transferring ideas constantly. Passive telepathy merely scoops these up, just like some-one listening to the radio who just switches on and then hears what is being sent out. No action is needed on the telepath, which is why it is referred to as passive telepathy.

This type of telepathy is most customarily connected to emerging ideas and, additionally, for someone with telepathic abilities. This skill can be challenging to switch off at first. Think of attempting to focus or sleep while someone in the next room turned a stereo to full volume, and you might have some concept.

Active telepathy otherwise requires the telepath to participate in a person's mind with specific intent and typically buries deeper to get at somewhat more concealed ideas and memories. This can feel very intrusive, and the subject might be acutely familiar with what is occurring.

Coercive telepathy describes a procedure by which a telepath will enter another's mind and change it somehow, possibly triggering them to think ideas that are not their own.

While many of the most experienced telepaths have been aware of their abilities the majority of, if not all, their lives, there are likewise many books, DVDs, and resources which aim to teach the development of telepathic capabilities to those of us who need a little guidance or are interested in mastering the ability.

Being an empath isn't simple. They're great listeners, yet they're sensitive too. There are chances for them to have drained on a physical and mental level. Thus, if somebody wants to share their feelings, next, it's best to enjoy them. But it's essential to plan boundaries and maintain space. Bear in mind, and if used well, empathy can be an excellent gift!

Chapter 8

How to Handle Your Empathy Without Getting Drained

Set Healthy Limits

For being naturally caring and worried for others, empaths have a difficult time stating "no." This can result in issues as you overcommit and deplete yourself emotionally. Controlling how much time you spend listening to difficult individuals, and learn to say 'no.' Set clear limitations and boundaries with individuals, nicely cutting them off at the pass if they get critical or indicate. Remember, 'no' is a total sentence.

Practice Mindfulness

Empaths require to book a time to tune in because they tend to get caught up in what is going on around them. Practicing caution can help you reconnect to yourself. Focusing on your breath, for persistence, quiets the mind and centers you in your body. It can be beneficial in meditation to practice "non-identification" with others, try to see yourself and your emotions as separate from anybody else's.

Neglect Your Inner Critic

The vital inner voice is like a nasty coach that lives inside our heads, waiting for any chance to slam us. Empaths, being sensitive, are susceptible to these self-critical ideas. They may believe things like, "Why do you feel a lot all the time? What's wrong with you?" or "You're simply too sensitive." Nevertheless, it is important not to think of these self-attacks or act upon your inner critic's lousy advice.

Practice Self-Compassion

While it is straightforward for empaths to feel compassion for others, it is frequently challenging for them to sympathize with themselves. Self-compassion is the natural (yet sturdy) practice of treating yourself like a good friend. Since it is something that you get much better at over time, it is called a method. There are three elements to practicing self-compassion:

1) Acknowledge and see your suffering.
2) One must be kind and caring in response to suffering.
3) Keep in mind that imperfection becomes part of the human experience and something we all share.

Spend Time In Nature

Nature has fantastic recovery effects for all people, but particularly for empaths. Author John Burroughs said, "I go to nature to be soothed and recovered, and to have my senses put in order." Since empaths are too conscious individuals (along with environments and noises) around them, time in nature is the optimum method for them to charge and unwind. Whether you live somewhere enables you to walk on the beach, hike through the woods, or sit in a park. It is necessary to renew in a beautiful, natural setting, especially when you are feeling overwhelmed or emotionally diminished.

At the end of our day, it is necessary to recognize both the proper blessings and empathizing difficulties. In a world where so many individuals struggle to identify and express emotions, empathy can look like a superpower. Welcome yours!

How An Empath Can Find Balance

Practice these methods to center yourself.

- Allow quiet time to decompress emotionally. Get in the habit of taking relaxing mini-breaks throughout the day. Breathe in some fresh air. Stretch. Take a brief walk around the workplace. These interludes will decrease the excessive stimulation of going non-stop.
- Practice guerilla meditation. To counter emotional overload, act quickly and meditate for a few minutes. This focuses your energy, so you do not take it on from others.
- Define and honor your empathic requirements. Protect your sensitivities. Here is how.
- If someone asks too much of you, nicely tell them "no." It's not necessary to describe why. As they say the word, "No" is a complete sentence.
- If your comfort level is 3 hours max for socializing-- even if you love the people-- take your automobile or have an alternate transport strategy, so you're not helpless.
- If crowds are overpowering, eat a high-protein meal in advance (this premises you) and sit in the far corner of, state, a theatre or celebration, not dead center.
- If you feel nuked by perfume, well, demand that your pals avoid using it around you. If you can't prevent it, stand near a window or take frequent breaks to catch a breath of fresh air outdoors.

- If you overindulge to numb unfavorable emotions, then practice the guerilla meditation mentioned above before you are tempted to the refrigerator, a potential vortex of temptation. As an emergency procedure, keep a cushion by the fridge so you can be poised to practice meditation instead of binge.
- Take private space in your home. Then you won't be stricken by the sensation of excessive togetherness.

In time, I suggest contributing to this list to keep yourself covered. You don't have to transform the wheel each time you're on emotional overload. With practical techniques to cope, empaths can have quicker retorts, feel more secure, and their talents can blossom.

Chapter 9

Tools For The Preservation Of Power Of An Empathy

Empaths are attracted to support themselves and others. You are usually attracted to healing because you feel you have so much inner healing unless, that is, they understand that for others, most of the healing they need is intuitively "feeling."

They are often in a constant state of tiredness. This is an enormous issue. Individuals and their energies continually steal the power of empathy.

An empath usually takes on too much and is drained quickly, and sleep or rest is not easily healed. It's much more profound and quite frustrating.

Empaths are excellent listeners. They genuinely care for others' welfare and hear people's woes they don't even know about. Empaths are so natural for most people to open up to. This is when they start to dump all kinds of negativity. Sometimes people don't even know that they do this.

In most situations, an Empathian cares well before his own for others' needs because they care so much. When people are comfortable enough to open around them, they usually give their hearing selflessly to help a person, even if it is detrimental.

Time alone is an empathy necessity. Most empaths like to remove all their feelings and power, so they need a lot of time apart. This is the time for them to regain balance and get away from all negative things that are not theirs.

The empath can also seem moody. Empathy often tends to have vast mood swings, which sometimes leads to all the conflicting thoughts and feelings surrounding them every day. Not only are they bombarded with these forces, but they also have to solve all this simply and find out.

We are prone to abuse, brutality, or any kind of disaster emotionally. Many empaths have stopped watching TV and reading newspapers at some point in their lives, too, for empathy.

Just plain knowledge is also a common feature of empathy. Empaths often know things that have been taught or told that they are right. This awareness is very distinct from instinct or intuition.

It is often daunting or unpleasant to be present in public places. Also, so many people's emotions can be swept up in public spaces if they don't. It is a roller coaster that most empaths avoid at all costs.

Empathy can 'sense' sincerity and completeness. You can say if somebody is honest or not, it is very troubling and sometimes painful in your life. It is particularly problematic when you work with your loved ones.

Feeling another's physical symptoms and pains. Most empaths will have a disease that somebody else has nothing to do with them. This is little empathy.

Crystals for Protecting your Energy

These are just some of the characteristics of an empath. Again, empathy can be regarded as a curse or a gift, depending on the instruments you use to protect yourself. Empaths can defend themselves in many ways. The avoidance of large social meetings or public spaces at any cost is one way. But sometimes you can't just avoid these things. There are many useful ways to protect yourself as empaths.

An excellent example is empathy crystals because its healing properties foster unconditional love and comfort. This is especially good for a person who has less caring energy than something, someone, or even herself.

Black tourmaline or hematite are also perfect crystals to sustain empathy. These stones also contribute to absorbing any negative energy.

Malachite is another mineral that tends to overcome negative feelings, whether you have them or not!

Labradorite is a crystal that protects your aura against any problems you share.

Citrine is a yellow crystal that allows the mood to shine. Another soothing property of Citrine is that it also helps to drain lousy energy from your surroundings.

Another one is Amethyst. It is not only good, but it will also reinforce your intuition. More significant intuition is excellent for all, but especially for Empaths, to help them know that their sensations may or may not have been theirs.

Rainbow Fluorite is last but not least. Rainbow Fluorite may be the Mother of all crystals for an empath, in my view, as it supports all stages of being! This multicolored crystal can help you remain grounded, clear, balance all chakras, and stay aligned with higher dimensions.

These are the crystals that help me to stay focused, safe, grounded, and tuned. Crystals can and will help your life to recover!

Meditation

For so long, meditation has been used to reach a consciousness level beyond the everyday thinking mind's limits. Simply put, it is the intention to bring the body, mind, and spirit together!

Most people do not understand that our bodies are designed to correct themselves to maintain positive health by balancing our whole well-being. Imagine how uncomplicated it is to be out of balance when other people's energy infiltrates your body every day. This is epic! It is grand!

If your energy in life flows out of balance, it doesn't flow as it should. Being out of balance in life shows up as pain and sorrow. And when your body becomes imbalanced for long enough, it begins to create disease and sickness.

Time and reflection alone are an excellent way for compassion to maintain balance, wellbeing, and dignity. This is the training of loving yourself that most Empaths put at the bottom of a line when they even emphasize it!

Many people do this differently, and there is no right or wrong way to do this because it is all about the power of intention.

Give yourself a few minutes and relax in a quiet place before you do anything. Close your eyes and breathe deeply. In every breath, imagine the white light of security that reaches your body through your crown and fills your whole being.

Try to breathe in the white light, and if your entire body is full of light, imagine that light is now brightly blinding and so tall that it now shines beyond you and covers your whole body. Sit quietly and enjoy the warmth that surrounds you for a few moments. Now smile and have a little gratitude because you have only practiced self-love first. And you just finished protecting yourself against every unwanted and harmful energy around you!

Chapter 10

The Secret Of Empath Psychic Capability

Sometimes it's hard to tell if somebody's a psychic with empathic skills. The dilemma is that you don't know if someone has such mental powers or just compassionate people who understand. How do you know?

Empathy is extremely sensitive to the feelings of the people around them. Often, a fellow can feel what someone is experiencing, even if they cannot see or hear him. Most psychics with empathic abilities say that they perceive others' emotions as if they were their own, but this is not always the case.

A psychic with such an ability can feel the feelings of others, especially when they are powerful. Frequent feelings of empathy include joy, fear, excitement, solitude, love, and forbidden news. The stronger the passion, the easier it will be for understanding to feel.

That separates empathy from other "natural" people. It is a more in-depth and more receptive perception of what they feel. This insight comes from within and is far higher than the opinions of most men. For example, an "average" person can know that somebody they love is upset by things they say or do. But empathy could feel that even without a person seeing or speaking, empathy could feel if that loved one felt upset, betrayed, or hurt. This psychic intuition would come from within, not from the physical world's visual and audible clues.

Empathy can tell when something is wrong, even if it didn't happen yet. We are profoundly discouraged and warned that not everything is as it should be. On the other hand, a "natural" person could not say if something unusual or dangerous would happen.

All these things sound great, but not everyone realizes that empathy can be complicated. This is because empathy cannot "shut down" their ability whenever they want. They can't choose to feel something or not. Instead, they have to feel whatever their psychic intuition feels, even if they don't. This is a considerable burden for empathy and also because of the exhaustion of empathic psychics.

What are empathic cognitive skills?

The empathic medium is also called "empathy." Empathies can perceive and understand other people's feelings, like how telepaths can sense other people's thoughts.

Empathy and telepathy are, in fact, closely related to mental abilities.

Typically clear-cut psychics have the empathic psychic ability (psychics with "clear sentiment"). Empathic qualities are uncommon but not unknown.

Empathy display these characteristics:

- Extreme sensitivity to others ' feelings
- A clear understanding of the language of their bodies:
- Awareness of their surroundings
- A deeper understanding of human emotion
- Empathic power is not all psychics.

Many psychics have rudimentary empathic abilities, and others have sophisticated empathic skills. Some empathies collapse in the middle somewhere.

Psychics with the popular basic empathic skills can feel what others feel. These psychics can be only knowing what others feel.

Psychics with advanced empathic abilities could feel all that others feel. As they exercise empathy, these psychics always get so deeply involved in people's feelings that they briefly lose sight of themselves. Psychics like these can send emotional signals and project their own opinions to others.

Most people choose to heal others with their strength. Empaths usually put their hands on someone to understand what they feel. Empathy can thus directly concentrate on what the patient needs.

Powerful empathic psychics can share other people's feelings to alleviate their pain. Loss and sadness are two universal emotions that a deep empathy will share and decrease. A psychic can also express his feelings to spread joy and happiness in reverse to this process.

A blessing or a curse?

Since empathy spends so much time worrying about other people's feelings, it can forget to worry. Empathy can suffer as a result of self-denial, emotional stress, and physical tiredness.

On the other hand, it is a rare and unusual gift to heal and spread joy!

What does that mean?

If you think you may have empathic psychic abilities, you must reveal your real supernatural power. If not, your empathic skills will never be useful! What a waste!

They are pretty intuitive people, more capable of reading people than "signs" or tarot cards. There are individuals of an empathic type, but this is just a small part of empathy.

They were very intuitive and could feel things that are unknown to the average person and inaccessible.

After 30 years of studying these forms, I concluded that they were lost and had the potential to "learn" things intuitively, like when someone wanted them to call, when someone had problems and needed help, or how to get there without ever getting here or following directions.

I concluded that these people had unprecedented changes to their central nervous systems (CNS). The communication between the CNS and the brain was so particular that a 'sixth sense' was developed, which received messages much more in-depth than "normal" persons and interpreted these messages unconventionally. Science has not yet evaluated the phenomenon. Many people have invested resources and time to study what empathy is.

Such studies have shown that empathic individuals have specific common qualities. Increased sensitivity is the most common denominator.

They are often labeled over-sensitive individuals, but perhaps a more suitable definition is ultra-sensitive.

They are highly sensitive to noise, smells, and light, and their sensory organs have a low threshold that amplifies the reaction of their senses.

In addition to these increased sensitivity levels, empathy is frequently bombarded by a constant flow of allegedly irrational thoughts and emotions. This is because they often "collect" others ' ideas and feelings, not just those nearby, but often people who are miles away, if not oceans apart. This is the mental makeup of an Empath, a disorder with which those who do not realize their gift battle. Because of the vast quantity of knowledge and the lack of understanding of its existence, most people become exhausted and confused, sometimes looking for psychological guidance or even medicine.

The simple explanation is that when a mental person "sees," an empathetic person "feels." The hunches and feelings of empathic personality experiences are psychic messages.

The problem with these messages is that they are communicated in a kind of psychic language that is foreign and complicated.

Are Empaths Rare?

Are Empaths uncommon? You can be forgiven for believing that they are all over, with numerous individuals declaring to be empaths these days. The majority of these people are mistaken, though they can be forgiven too. A lot of them are just empathic, which is not the same thing as being an empath. There are numerous resemblances between these two groups of people, but they are not two separate groups. Every empath is compassionate, but not everybody who is empathic is also an empath.

What separates the empathic ability is in the difficult and physical processes that accompany the emotional reaction. Put in simpler terms: a compassionate person can imagine how they would feel in another individual's shoes, whereas an empath more excellent feels it.

They do not experience their feelings as though they remained in the same scenario. They take advantage of the other individual's emotional energy and feel like they are feeling them.

This difference is extremely subtle, but it is also extremely powerful. Our experience of life, from our viewpoint, is completely subjective. No matter how hard we attempt, the large bulk of us will just reveal our own experience. For those uncommon few, their experience of life consists of the experiences of others. Since they are inexperienced, doing it is totally out of their control. It is both a gift and a curse. These things can not be said about compassionate individuals. The issue with separating these two groups is that our language is restricted.

How an empathic person explains their skills and how an empath describes theirs are often really comparable. Since the limitations of language, the experience is defined the same way. An expert empath can generally inform the real deal from an empathic person.

How Rare Are Empaths?

Empathic individuals comprise about 15-20% of the population-- around 1 in 7 individuals. Empaths, meanwhile, just add up to about 2% of the population-- roughly 1 in 50 people.

We have to take those numbers with a pinch of salt.

They are rough quotes based on specialists' experiences in the field, so they are necessarily based on limited sample sizes. This implies that the number of Empaths could be much lower, though it is unlikely it would be much greater.

Are Empaths unusual? Yes.

How rare are Empaths? Not vanishingly so.

In a town of 10,000 individuals, there would be 200 of them. You most likely understand a couple of them, a minimum of in passing. If there are multiple people in your good friend group claiming to be empaths, the opportunities are extremely slim that more than one of them is. Possible, but it is highly not likely.

If you reside in a great city, you might understand a number of these people!

Among the benefits of residing in a huge city is that there are similar individuals somewhere around. There are flourishing communities in many cities worldwide, and, naturally, they would gravitate towards each other. A higher degree of emotional receptivity is needed for men before they can declare this status. Are male Empaths rare? Yes, specifically so. But they do exist!

There are likewise fewer empathic males. It is a problem in the broader society.

A lack of balance between manly and womanly energies has instilled itself in culture, causing numerous men not interacting with their feelings effectively. The sad thing is that this is fixable, and it would be of terrific advantage.

Are Male Empaths Rare?

Viewing as the answer to "are Empaths rare?" is yes, it appears evident that they would be, and you are right. However, exactly how rare are empaths who are male?

Female energies are much more associated with social thinking, psychological connection, and empathy than male energies.

While most people have a reasonable balance between feminine and masculine energies, women tend to have more feminine energy. Men tend to have more masculine energy. It's not always the case and should not be taken as a rule; however, it is important when we speak about statistics.
So females are most likely to have a better connection with empathy and are, for that reason, more likely to be empathic. The more individuals who are empathic, the more people there are that could be empathic.

Male empaths are unusual because there are less strongly empathic guys.

The Anxiety of Being Empathic

How often did you feel confused or think later in the day that one of your loved ones has a similar experience? Maybe that person had emotionally tricky things, but you experienced the symptoms? What about the pain that just happens and goes unexpectedly for a while? Once again, you will find out that a beloved has some physical pain, yet the symptoms have been experienced. Odd, is it? How did you find out that your wife was experiencing changes? Have you rejected your experience as a strange phenomenon?

The reality is none of the above is as weird or unusual as you might imagine. If you have ever felt thoughts or physical symptoms of other beings, you are considered an empath.

Empathy is defined as intellectual recognition or vicarious experience of another's feelings, thoughts, or attitudes. An empath is, however, someone who energetically absorbs others' feelings, beliefs, or attitudes.

Empathy must NOT be in a person's physical presence to experience these experiences. Most people who are empathic can not determine their thoughts, feelings, or attitudes. They mistake these emotions and beliefs and can carry them unknowingly throughout their lives.

So what's the big thing about it? Let's look at this in several ways, and then let's see how you feel when you finish the book.

Empath Examples

You are a child that is taunted by the children in your school about stupid things. As a result, you don't really like school, and you have little self-esteem. The school experience affects you so much that a conviction is thereby formed.

You establish this belief as a means of coping and emotional security. The knowledge may be so "Others don't accept it," "I'm not worthy of friendship," "I don't deserve friendships," or "I don't love myself." That one conviction produces most heirs that replicate themselves.

These myriad creeds are now in your subconscious mind, and you are currently carrying it throughout your adult life. You also have the feelings, emotional expressions, and opinions that caused all the kids to do and tell you what they did. You have merged emotionally and mentally with them.

Another example: you have negative thoughts always. You are critical, judicious, and skeptical. The thing is that you know that it's not the right thing, but you can't change things no matter what you do.

Nothing works, no matter what you do. People say you're very pessimistic, and you don't like it, but you can't figure out why you are like that. In this case, a few things are more than likely to happen.

First of all, you may have merged empathically with certain situations in life that have made you react badly. Also, because of the location, your subconscious has been formed with negative beliefs. What is most popular is the person who has the empathy was exposed to another person who is very bad or has even "inherited" the negativity of a family person.

This usually only transmits negative thinking empathetically or energetically and can be immediately removed.

It is natural for us to relate and to be able to communicate in our lives. The actual symptoms of the challenges of others are not healthy or balanced. It is a human trait to be compassionate during difficult times. We often want to help someone else by easing the pain, and guess what?

You might have done that before. Have ever discussed with someone who's been going through rough times, and afterward, when the conversation is over, they say, "Huh! Glad I've got it off my chest. I'm feeling so much better!"

Hey, you just swallowed everything like that person's an emotional sponge. In reality, you didn't take the pain away, just the weight of their load. Later on, when they come again to speak about their issue, you find that talking to them about what they are doing is increasingly difficult. This is because the person's negative emotions are like weighing down the flow of positive energy.

There's a lot of empathy. Many people can not even leave home because just the combination of feelings in the air induces vomiting, fatigue, or nervousness. Others can go home, but note that they retain their bodies' negative symptoms when they touch people and then find a way to relieve them.

No matter how timely or extreme individuals' empathic abilities are, they must be all regulated.

You have many people who think empathy is refreshing, while some think it's a curse. No matter what you believe, you don't have to feel the other person's physical symptoms.

You may actively choose only to collect information to help the other person. If this pure awareness doesn't work, you may need to remove certain faiths and emotions on the subconscious level that will influence your life.

Chapter 11

Empathy and Empaths

Empathy means one must be in tune with other people's sensations and life scenarios. An empathetic person might be affected by a circumstance in a sort of heart-tugging, emotional manner that ultimately generates kind, caring, and comprehending words and actions. For instance, it pertains to extending a suitable reaction when someone loses a task or revealing enjoyment when a pal reveals her pregnancy-- even if both are scenarios that may have never affected you personally.

An article mentions that "empathy" is "a rendering of the German Einfühlung" or a "sensation into" that involves the "ethical implications of feeling our method into other's lives."

Then there is being what they called an empath, which refers to someone who takes empathy a significant action further. An empath can take and feel other individuals' emotions as if they experience those sensations themselves.

Can you conclude that having empathy usually implies you're an empath? After all, lots of understanding individuals feel deeply for other individuals' setbacks and successes. Does this make them an empath?

The short answer: Yes, and no.

However, an Empath's essence has something to do with empathy, yet, on an entirely more profound level. In short, empaths feel on a stronger level than understanding people.

The Contrast Between Empathy and Being an Empath

It separates between "regular empathy" in which an individual's heart heads out to another and being an empath, in which those feelings belong on a much wider spectrum. Empaths not only feel for others but soak up those sensations in their system.

Besides, empaths can often detect unmentioned sensations and use subtle energy fields that emanate around other people's bodies. Energy absorption takes place, and a secure noticing experience begins. Depending on the kind of energy-- whether around a joyful, delighted individual or an afraid, anxiety-ridden individual-- an empath will feel deeply, frequently experiencing shifts in mood and energy levels.

This begs the query of how an empath can take care of themselves. After all, in addition to experiencing their feelings, they are absorbing other individuals' feelings. This can take a toll on them, specifically in scenarios that leave them drained pipes. It is not uncommon for empaths to experience many physical signs as they take on many intense feelings, consisting of stomach and headaches.

Empathy is the incredible fabric of relatedness and, therefore, the material of our ability to reside in communication with life itself.

Real empathy is a state of being when we live empathically. We can relate to our full experience of life at a level of mindful awareness. Awareness of oneself, awareness of others, and higher universal intelligence awareness are vibrant and integral.

Suppose our task as grownups are to reach a state of healthy autonomy with ownership. An awareness of the authority of both our ideas and our subsequent choices and actions, then we will need to deepen and establish our self-awareness. We will require to discover to listen to ourselves.

When I talk about empathy, I see it as a listening skill and something that we can offer to others. If we wish to live and browse our lives from a prospering self-responsibility position, we will need to establish a growing relationship with ourselves. 'A relationship of depth and significance.'

We are becoming progressively knowledgeable about our remarkable mind's power and impact in co-creating our journey throughout our lives. Several books and clinical studies connect both the science and the spirituality of energy, and, undoubtedly, our human capacity for conscious option and influence within this sphere.

Nevertheless, based on my experience. The area of our lives in which the majority of people struggle is connected to feeling. When we are stressed out or too emotionally charged, our emotions color our understandings, which, in turn, colors our thinking and, therefore, our following choices.

It has been my advantage to walk alongside literally hundreds of people as they have traveled from the mayhem of living from an emotionally reactive position. They are going to a place of incorporated living, where their feelings fuel and feed their capability to browse their lives from a position of conscious and reflective choice. And it is the secret to producing this level of change is empathy.

How Empaths Can Look After Themselves

Compare Your Feelings and Everybody Else's.

Empaths need to take a step back when interacting with others to determine whether their feelings originate from their feelings or others' feelings. I always ask patients to ask themselves, 'Is the feeling mine or that of another individual?'. It's necessary to learn more about and listen to your body. They are acknowledging how you feel in the past and after interactions are crucial.

Enjoy Being an Empath.

Sure, you are soaking up a great deal of feeling in addition to managing your own. However, that is frequently an advantage. I would not quit being an empath for anything.

Empaths are typically filled with generosity. Empaths are talented. They feel a deep connection to animals and the earth, form deep friendships, delight in nature, and worth intimate discussions. Empaths are nurturing people who enjoy assisting others and want to see other individuals delighted.

It is recommended not to focus on the many negative misconceptions that typically surround empaths. Such as people who state they are "being too delicate" or require to establish a "thicker skin.".

Accept who you are and neglect negative words from other people who might not completely comprehend and appreciate how you experience things so profoundly.

However, Understand Harmful Relationships and Other

Issues.

While empaths enjoy assisting others, in some cases, people-pleasing behaviors establish, or they become codependent.

One typical relationship I see the form is between an empath and a narcissist. A narcissist, who battles with empathy deficit condition, gravitates towards those who supply and nurture attention. At the same moment, an empath falls for the appeal of a narcissist who ultimately ends up being cold and restraining. Narcissists are especially effective at gaining the affection and appreciation of others. Might also leave a trail of broken relationships behind them as soon as they have been learned.

The caring nature makes them genuinely want to recover that cold, uncaring character, creating an ongoing, unbalanced emotional cycle between the two.

Research reveals that we generally feel more empathy for our group members, such as our ethnic group. We do not always feel empathy for those who are not members of our group. Another barrier to expressing authentic empathy is the propensity to believe that we are responsible for making other people feel much better, particularly those we love. Empathy suggests being in tune with other people's sensations and life situations. We need both, not one at the expenditure of the other. Empathy sits at the core of our ability to engage with life, from both our hearts and our mind.

Set Limits, Practice Self-Care

It prevails for empaths to be overly polite and want others to be so delighted that they sacrifice their well-being. Engage and set healthy limits in time management strategies like not overbooking yourself. Try meditation practices every day to relax and center yourself, and make sure to go out in nature frequently too. Nature offers a connection with animals and the earth that is not shallow; she keeps in mind, which helps restore a sense of calm.

Connect with Other Empaths

Take pleasure in connecting with other empaths from the comfort of your own home. When you join an empath group, you can chat with other empaths, understand their experience, ask concerns, and participate in intriguing discussions.

In other words, empaths often absorb energy from other individuals, experiencing feelings on a level beyond empathy. While being an empath can be pleasurable, it is essential to take the time to practice self-care, compare your feelings with others, and connect with other empaths.

So how do you understand what your energies are and what they are not?

Among the best methods is to take a look at how your energy is before you leave home. To see your mood, how your body feels, what ideas are coming up, generally check your entire emotional, mental. Physical states to see how they are. When you start to step out into the world, blending with all the other energies of other people, you will start to feel different or your mood all of a sudden unexplainably modified. Alternatively, you feel unpleasant physical sensations, and then you understand you are selecting up 'outside' energies.

Chapter 12

The Psychology of Empathy

Empathy is an integral part of emotions and a particular emotion involving a feeling component of interaction and a physical reaction of verbal or nonverbal communication at the stages of empathy and the need for an empathy dependent therapy model. In general, empathy means to feel what the other person feels and "to be in the shoes of the other person." Empathy establishes emotional connections and contact between partners, family, acquaintances, and even strangers. Empathy concerns connectivity and a sense of knowing what another person feels. Many people are simply more empathic than others, while some people may find it difficult to relate. Psychology should answer some issues that cause empathy and why some individuals are more empathic than others.

Empathy or empathy and being in others' shoes are closely linked to intuition, as intuition helps people understand and perceive emotions. Even if feelings are hidden and not expressed, empathy helps to identify them through intuition. Insight is, therefore, defined as the awareness of others' emotions through intuition and is characterized by a sense of connection with the other.

In any leadership circumstance, such as political leadership and social leadership, leaders feel an affinity with the other group members. Leaders have to be associated with followers to influence their views and decisions. Teachers must also have empathy towards the students because this provides a bond in which both the teaching experience and the students are meaningless. Empathy is about inspiring or manipulating others by stimulating their emotions. If you are well aware of what they think or feel, it is easier to influence or change people as this helps to anticipate possible responses. Ultimately, we only understand others if we can anticipate their reactions, and empathy brings their interactions a predictive value.

Stages of Empathy

Empathy may begin with intuition and predict that one person can predict another's emotional responses. The step of empathy is as follows: 1. Take Intuition 2. Connection 3. Recital 4. Prediction 5. Motivation. The first phase of intuition includes one person instinctively intuitive to the other. It creates the next level of empathy or feeling of connectedness to the intuition of another person's emotions and feelings or processes of thought. The relationship between two people gives rise to a sense of mutual concern and predicting the responses. In some instances, empathy can be reciprocal, although understanding can be side-by-side in many cases, as in a relationship between a therapist and her patient. After the relationship has been established and the other person's feelings have a profound sense of consideration and an understanding of why they feel in a certain way, a person who has sympathy can move to the next stage to predict emotional response. Learning other people's reaction habits is an essential element for communicating and comparing them carefully and will imply the opportunity to be in another's shoes. The last steps of empathy deal with the more relational dimension. It is essential to inspire or affect another person after an empathic relation with an instructor or counselor. Yes, empathy has been developed to manipulate the other person to accomplish different objectives or goals. Therefore, the other person's power and motivation are an integral part of empathy and an implicit goal of empathic relations.

In contrast to the five phases of empathy, empathy could include feelings of respect, affection, intimacy, appreciation, and dependency. This depends on whether insight is between a lecturer and an individual, a psychologist and a leader, a client, and those that are following him between friends or lovers.

Psychologically, compassion will include addressing other people's safety and security needs and their needs for affection and association.

Therefore, empathy needs to lie somewhere between the love-based (psychological) needs of persons' safety needs. There is a need for empathy in all people, and both forms of empathy are manifested.

Individuals meet their needs for love and affiliation about others, and empathy uses love and attachment to ensure safety and security. Thus, as Maslow's hierarchy of need theory has explained, compassion aims to make the other person happy by providing security and lending support as empathy could have a positive influence on the other person. Empathy significantly improves social interaction by incorporating familiarity, relations, and trust between people and instilling and preserving human values.

Theory and therapy

In addition to Maslow's basic requirements, the concept of empathy could be utilized successfully by any psychotherapeutic framework and a treatment pattern based on the affecting interaction between the therapist and the client. Every client-centered therapy requires empathic linkages between the customer and the therapist and the evolution of a Therapeutic System, on the ICCPM model (Intuition, connection, prediction-motivation).

It could be a therapeutic method that identifies and evokes various phases of empathy between the customer and therapist to reach the therapist.

For instance, if a customer suffers from depression, the Therapeutic Affective Framework can use ICCPM to emphasize that the customer interacts with the therapist intuitively. This is only after the psychologist obtains a history or experience of the psychological condition or client's illness. The intuitive stage in which a client and counselor establish an unconscious connection is accompanied by linking the client to the therapist and making interaction simple.
The third phase is considered both the patient and the psychologist agree to collaborate for a specific purpose. The fourth stage of psychological interaction is based on the fact that both the client and therapist can anticipate responses and replies and empathize with each other's thoughts.

The therapy's last stages focus on decision-making and assessment to see if the patient's motivational level has been changed and whether the psychologist has affected the client's actions or thought process.

The Love Psychology

The psychological foundation of love originates in a fundamental process called 'attachment,' which is the close relationship between child and caregiver that begins at birth. Devotion is not confined to mankind.

A baby chick or gosling can be observed to attach to the first organ after birth, generally his mother. The baby's going to follow the mother anywhere. This phenomenon is not learned behavior, known as "imprinting" in animals. The chicks are neurologically conditioned for this response. The movie "Fly home" portrayed a ghost story of a young boy. In mammals, a more complex relationship occurs between mother and child so that everyone is related to the other.

Psychologists believe that human love starts with a newborn child's earliest attachment to his mother. The child is born with the reflex to suck, which initiates the attachment process. The first answer is unlearned, but the child soon learns to combine milk, warmth, proximity, touch, and comfort. If a mother has problems-if, she has little or no milk or is depressed or anxious- there may be issued with the bonding process.

A stressed mother transmits this pressure to her baby. The baby will develop colic, get agitated, and eat hard, even with a bottle. This raises the stress of the wife. In worse situations, the mother can be severely disturbed, dependent on alcohol or drugs, and the baby can be rejected. Neglect, violence, or abandonment can occur. The kid might be placed in a shelter or hospital if no substitute care is available. Loss of primary care at an early age can have serious consequences. Children can develop disorders of attachment. They may have difficulty trusting others or forming relationships. They may lack the ability to love.

In the absence of their mothers, psychologists identified three types of attachments in infants and examined how they act and what happens when they return. Children with healthy attachments frequently explore their world in their parents' presence but consistently use it as a safe foundation before investigating. They get agitated at long distances.

Children with less secure, worrying attachments are also looking to their mother for closeness. When the mother comes back after an absence, she is angry and not comforted by her presence. A third reaction is considered a mysterious connection. When the mother comes home after an absence, the child rejects her completely. The type of attachment pattern of a child seems to be associated with the behavior of the mother. Mothers of children with healthy attachments are sensitive to their feelings and appropriately respond to their needs. Mothers of children with emotional attachments seem to be worried about themselves and return to the infant's feelings incoherently. Children's mothers with avoiding attachments often ignore their children and can reject their comfort needs.

Attachment behaviors during adolescence may also be related to later behavioral patterns. Many people have no difficulty getting close to another person and are comfortable in relationships. They are not worried that they will be abandoned. In the absence of a loved one, they will believe and are less lonely.

If you feel stressed, you can come to others for comfort. If someone else is stressed, they can offer support. You can share your feelings with others. People with anxiety are often confused about their relationships. You want to be close to another person, but you don't believe your feelings are returned. They're concerned about rejection. They engage in relationships between love and hate. They are actively establishing and breaking ties. They have low self-appreciation. Less likely are avoiding lovers to enter into relationships. They don't feel comfortable approaching or allowing others to contact them. They may have casual relations, but they can go as far as they can. You can not express your thoughts. We explain the rejection of their family.

Psychologists have also studied the empathy process.
 Some behavioral scientists have suggested that empathy as a species is critical for our survival. It seems to be born and maybe, like attachment, one of the earliest manifestations of love.

When a newborn baby hears another baby's cry, it also starts crying. The baby's reaction to another person's discomfort is not just an answer to loud noise. David Hoffman, a New York

University psychologist, claims that the unlearned response is the start of empathy, the ability to watch and recognize another person's feelings. This emotional response allows us to survive and help others. Empathy includes feelings and the thoughts an empathic person must feel like someone else feels and must understand why.

Empathy is a process of development in children. In the beginning, children can not differentiate themselves from others. Nevertheless, babies begin to distinguish between themselves and others by the end of their first year.

When a baby hears another baby crying, he knows that he doesn't have trouble himself. Nevertheless, the baby always shows anxiety.
Nonetheless, he now has stronger coping strategies. He can use the same procedure to comfort the other child, like bringing a teddy bear to the distressed child and bringing it into a comfortable mother. At the end of the second year, a child realizes that everyone has their inner feelings. By the age of five, the child understands that social situations will disturb people. While biological predispositions to empathy certainly exist, the environment is essential. There are vast differences between individuals. Maternal warmth appears to increase understanding. Moms who communicate clear messages to their children about the consequences of hurting others also have more empathic children. Individuals are more compassionate to and attracted to people whom they see themselves as close. Women have more sympathy for men, and women have more empathy with women. People are more sympathetic to their group members than to members of higher or lower classes. Empathy continues to grow throughout one's life and is undoubtedly an essential part of falling into love.

Psychology and Schizophrenia

The chronic, persistent, damaged brain disease is Psychology and Schizophrenia. It can indeed be described as a disorder characterized by various cognitive and emotional dysfunctions, involving general impaired thought, language and communication skills, perception, and fluency in thinking and talking and interpersonal functioning. More often, it affects the ability of a person to "think straight." Thoughts come and go quickly and easily, and a person may not focus on one idea for a very long time and maybe distracted.

Persons with schizophrenia often undergo or have frightening hallucinations symptoms. In general, psychotic symptoms tend to smell, watch, listen, or feel something that doesn't exist in a hallucination. However, they may also have an incorrect sense of sound, like listening to different sounds or voices that other individuals may not hear.

These are the most common psychotic symptoms, affecting about 65% to 70% of patients. Therefore, delusion is a false mental belief, and a person often believes that other people read or manipulate the mind. Such signs can make them scary. In many situations, their language and actions are so disorganized that they can be impenetrable or intimidating for others.

In addition to this person who has schizophrenia, severe mental symptoms, or even insanity, can also be encountered because of undetected critical medical conditions. A client may not be able to sort out the issue irrelevantly or adequately. The patient may not be able to connect thoughts into coherent sentences, with thoughts disordered and scattered. However, an individual may be interested in social activities, avoid contact with others, and may not have had anything to say when forced to cooperate.

In some serious situations, someone can spend almost a whole day doing nothing. Such alarming speech disorders can be especially disturbing to friends or even family members. In any event, the disease's consequences are extraordinarily emotional, and psychological treatments can help and are one of the best ways to treat it.

The use of cognitive-conduct therapy, mostly known as psychotherapy, has recently shown positive changes in both positive and negative symptoms in some patients. The technique has improved the patient's ability to think naturally through mental exercise and self-observation. There was some evidence that patients have even significantly increased their ability to learn and remember different things. Besides, individual psychotherapy is another form of psychosocial therapy for schizophrenia patients. This therapy focuses primarily on current or previous feelings, problems, experiences, thoughts, and relationships.

A client shares his experience with an educated, empathetic person in this therapy. It can help the patient think more about themselves and their issues and talk about their lives outside. This psychotherapy allows them to find a way of distorting the authentic and imaginary universe. Studies also show that supportive, reality-oriented people's psychotherapy can be a benefit for schizophrenic patients.

Schizophrenia psychotherapy also emphasizes bringing structure to the life of a person. This process can help the patient with schizophrenia work every day, maintain good personal hygiene, and develop personal relations.

Astro-Psychology Self Comprehension

Astrology approaches human nature psychology by studying and analyzing the divine forces and energies of the solar system, zodiac, and planets throughout the entire human psyche.

Science is based on the old paradigm and its strong and conventional research based on health factors, character, human relations, circumstances, and national and broader issues affecting our world.

Astro-psychology simply begins with the serious consideration of the zodiacal sign of birth in its study of individual human nature. We learn to identify the positive features defined by 'our mark' and find it easy to agree that we share these virtues. The attention to the negative traits is not so simple, but equally important. Although often shared as inherent weaknesses in all of us, they are especially evident in us and others with the same sign of birth.

In assessing these excellent or evil tendencies or traits, we must understand that we may not have learned or wish to express this particular characteristic of our birth sign personally. In this case, they remain specific energies or resources to easily access when we choose to use them.

Our free will determines our way of life and enables us to go along the more accessible roads and roads that astrology can indicate or choose a path from the route. The decision is always ours, regardless of what a subtle influence in the starry heavens' weather. However, as the farmer makes hay wisely when the sun shines, some activities and efforts are more likely to succeed when the planetary climate leads to productive results. Therefore we continue to be aware of the 'atmosphere of the sky' in addition to earthly weather patterns.

The advantages of learning all zodiacal signs and their defects and virtues, including ours, are to broaden our understanding and recognize the differences in human nature in our people. It's a smart practice with excellent results.

We are encouraged to study the nature of the zodiacal signs and their effects on planetary energies and, ultimately, on our conditions, moods, and behaviors.

We find that planetary movements lead to ever-changing patterns of their influence more volatile than the standard powers emitted from the twelve segments zodiac of the world. The aspects of relationships between one planet and another at any given time create complex or harmonious combinations of energy patterns to which we will respond.

Just as psychology has developed some basic rules and prevalent factors in human nature and behavior, which offer us a sense of common ground with others, astrology as a philosophy is complex to indicate why we are as we are. This applies in all areas of our being and our shared goal of self-development and excellence in physical, emotional, intellectual, and spiritual achievement.

When our diagram is drawn up, attention is also paid to natural elements known as water, earth, air, and fire, determining the proportion of these characteristics: practical, emotional, intellectual, or spiritual. This is related to the celestial position of these elements in zodiacal signs.

The study of astrology has many excellent benefits. Many are practical, such as planting crops while moon phases, preparing social programs, predicting fishing outcomes, finding a compatible partner or companion for healing, or choosing a suitable date for key national events. Astrologers decide to specialize in many possible applications.

However, using and implementing what we learn about human nature through Astro psychology's art gives us a fascinating interest. It enables us to feel inwardly comfortable, knowing that we form part of an endless variety of nature through its creative design, which uniquely expresses itself, but at the same time allows us to feel part of a broader human family. In this world, we are soothing and empathizing with at least one-twelfth of the billions, with whom we will always feel a special bond by the mutual zodiacal influences that we have at birth.

A straightforward and rational approach is suggested so that we fail in believing the stars are controlling us in a way that overrides free will. We also do not want extreme self-affirmation so that all forces of great nature are questioned or blamed rather than abused.

In addition to shared characteristics, we each have a unique nature, with a specific intent and life skills. Watching and understanding this unique nature allows us to experience a renewed sense of self-confidence and enhance our desire to live in a playful, creative way and with a unique gift to the world.

Nice! Almost done!

Hi there!

You got through a lot of information until now! I'm happy you got to this point, close to get to the end of the book, I hope you are liking what you read!

As you are now more aware of the valuable information inside this book, I'd like to kindly ask for your support with leaving a review on Amazon. It would only take 30 seconds of your time but it would make a huge difference to me, and it would help other people like you finding some valuable insights on the topic they are interested in.

>>You can Leave a Review Here<<

Or Scan This Code With your Phone Camera

If you have any feedback, please get in touch with me at the following contacts, I have them at the beginning of the book, but for your convenience I drop them here too!

Website: sharoncopeland.com

Email: info@sharoncopeland.com

Facebook Page: https://swiy.io/SharonCopelandFBPage

Facebook Support Book:
https://swiy.io/SharonCopelandFBGroup

Instagram: @saroncopelandauthor

Happy Reading!

Chapter 13

Emotional Intelligence

Understanding

We all know general intelligence, but how many of us are familiar with Emotional Intelligence? Emotional Intelligence is the ability to recognize, empathize, implement, and positively handle emotions to communicate effectively, relieve pressures, overcome difficulties, appreciate others, and smartly resolve conflicts.

In the physical sciences and sociology, it has since become a buzz word. Smooth skill subsystems and trainers reiterate the importance of emotional intelligence in working environments and social situations.

Emotional intelligence, even more than intellectual capacity, is required to gain success and happiness in life. Sensitive information is helpful in work, career development, relationships, and personal objectives. From here on, Emotional Intelligence is referred to as EQ.

How do you increase your EQ? You will improve your EQ by studying and developing a few essential skills: first, you must know that your emotions affect different aspects of daily life the way you live, the way you behave, and the way you communicate with others. With a high EQ, you can recognize your own and another emotional state. This knowledge helps you to communicate and persuade others to draw them closer to you. The success with which you can use your EQ leads to success throughout your life, leading to more life satisfaction.

Emotional intelligence has four principal qualities and characteristics: "Knowing yourself is the beginning of all wisdom," said Aristotle. This knowledge holds the key to developing your EQ further.

Self-consciousness: Have you ever stopped thinking about who you are? Is it good or bad, witty or severe, smart or dull, etc.?

Well, if you sit there and look at yourself as an outsider, you may understand the real "you." If you look deeply, you can understand why, in certain circumstances, you acted in specific ways. The ability to look at yourself is self-conscious. Self-awareness helps you identify your thoughts, weaknesses, strengths, values, actions, fears, feelings, and the whole 'you'. You can speak to your loved ones and friends in addition to yourself to make you understand. You can receive feedback from those who give you their honest views. It determines, to some degree, how others view you. This is done in marketing through a questionnaire on the product and performance of a company.

This is evaluated and used to improve the products and services of the company. You could also ask your dear ones to assess you and understand and improve your EQ in areas that you lack from their responses. As an adult, you can do this in the form of a newspaper.
Journaling is indeed a great way to see what you are and what your real feelings are. If you have a high level of EQ, you are more in contact with your own emotions. In turn, this enhances your confidence in life, yourself, and others.

Self-management: self-consciousness leads to self-control.

Everything about self-management is about managing your thoughts and acts. You control yourself by impulsive conduct. Openness, performance, adaptability, and optimism are developed. How do you respond to some situations? Should you respond to people and circumstances or react to them? It's a small difference, but there's a significant difference in meaning in practice. In EQ, reaction and response play an important role.

For example, if you have to wait a busy day for the traffic to move so slowly, are you impatient? Do you shout at other drivers and horns or wait for traffic to clear? Were you listening to or responding to heavy traffic? If you are impatient, you react emotionally to traffic.
If you react, you tend to lose reason. On the other hand, you are patient and, therefore, more comprehensive and reflective. After all, at some point, the traffic must continue! Self-management means adaptability, performance transparency, and optimism.

Social consciousness: Your self-awareness and self-management take you to the next step in social awareness.

You are open to understanding other people's feelings, desires, and concerns. You can gain emotional insights, feel socially relaxed, and recognize the power play within a group or organization. You need to see and hear others in their shoes to grow the EQ. Those with superior social intelligence have a greater sense of responsibility, compassion, and organizational understanding. These are the main characteristics of social awareness. Social awareness offers a natural response to people, taking into account their situation and needs. You can consider your EQ to be high if you exhibit these qualities.

Relationship management: Relationship management is the final area that you need to improve in growing your EQ.

We can look at this feature concerning your profession. This is your EQ aspect, which allows you to inspire others and help them achieve their full potential. It is also essential to negotiate, resolve conflicts, and work with others towards a shared objective.

Your success in this final area depends directly on your success in the other three regions, as management is concerned with interacting successfully with other people. Is not effective management doing the job?

• Leadership–cultivate others by recognizing their strengths; motivating others probably by your encouragement
• being a catalyst for progress to incorporate new ideas if the change is necessary
• Conflict management
• networking
• Communication
• teamwork and collaboration
• giving credibility

How does your life influence emotional intelligence?

Work performance-EQ lets you manage interpersonal challenges in a comfortable way, inspire, and lead others in your career. Nowadays, companies consider emotional intelligence to be an essential aspect and administer EQ assessments before recruiting.

Physical well-being-Stress is imminent in the world today, regardless of the profession. Stress is a known factor that leads to serious health problems in most people. Uncontrolled stress levels raise the risk of cardiovascular disease. When the stress level is high, our immune system suffers.

Mental well-Being-Stress negatively affects mental health. You may have read or heard of depressed people committing suicide. In the absence of emotional control, you become victims of mood swings or other mental disorders that seldom allow you to form or maintain healthy relationships in life.

Personal relationships-Your senses help you communicate the emotions to your loved ones. When communication is blocked, your relationships suffer at work and in your own lives.

Here are the tips for enhancing emotional understanding:

- Learn how to decrease negative feelings
- Stay cool and manage stress
- Be strong and voice painful opinions when necessary
- Stay proactive and not reactive in challenging situations
- Bounce back from adversity
- Express intimate emotions in close, personal relationships.

In this time, Emotional Intelligence (EQ) is an art to intelligently address your emotions in any life situation. This ability paves the way for success and self-confidence in every aspect of your life.

Chapter 14

Create Empathy

Empathy is the creative projection into an entity of a subjective state to infuse the object. It is also the practice of knowing, being sensitive to, and vicarious with the emotions, being conscious of, thoughts and experience of someone else from the past or the present, without having to articulate the feelings, thoughts, and experience fully; also: the ability to do so for empathy is an essential life skill.

In most walks of life, you should find success. It allows you to experience many different perspectives that are essential to your personal development and understanding. Empathy is, in an opinion, the one critical ability to transform the world and to create the sort of societies we are all thinking about.

Empathizing involves thriving in the opposite sex. You can become a strong, expressive speaker through empathy. You can become a prominent businessman and generally achieve many of the things you intend to do in your life.

This is because compassion helps you to consider what the other person is thinking about. It enables you to know others' desires, so you can do your best to meet them. If you are an entrepreneur, you can understand what the customer wants, and you will achieve success by fulfilling those needs. As a lover, sometimes before they know it themselves, you will know your partner's needs, which will make you the best lover they ever had.

You will be safe to empathize with your community and the people around you. By understanding other people's intentions, you will be able to avoid those that harm you. You can also learn to sympathize with a geographical area so that all signs that can warn you of dangers can be read subconsciously. Through compassion, you will learn to avoid the hazardous alley or stay away from an individual building or car.

Empathy is also going to make you a better, imaginative person. Remember the famous saying, "Walk a mile in other man's moccasins," before judging him.

This is sound advice that will help you gain insight into someone else's viewpoint so that you can appreciate their emotions, actions, and motives.

The ability to empathize is the ability to get beyond your ego. Another way to say this is to say that compassion allows the ego to grow to see with different eyes.

Place yourself comfortably before the crop. A house plant is perfect, but you can always sit outside in a quiet area in front of a bush or trees if you do not have one. You want to put yourself in a position to look at the plant comfortably. Hopefully, you will be indoors in a quiet room or outdoors in a beautiful place where you will be calm and unruly.

Next, you'll want to look at the crop gently. Slowly start to concentrate exclusively on the plant before you from this light glance. Try to see the plant without strain. In other words, you claim to know the plant and its inner spirit.

This workout takes several fantastic leaps. Those imaginative springs should be done without pressure. Rather than any kind of work, think of them as a child's pretending game.

When you look into the soul of the plant, imagine that you feel the tug from the plant to connect your soul and the soul of the plants. This connection, which feels like a small, almost surreal tug inside, allows you to ship a piece of yourself into the plant directly.

You are now imaginatively entering the plant with a short thread. A thin thread is one with the plant so that you now know you are and the crop.

You are now, and you are the vine, too. Imagine how do you experience the world around you as a plant? Try to explore what the plant feels right now with your imagination.

Plants have no eyes, but they can feel the world around them in the most incredible way. Plants are exceptionally temperately, psychologically, and humidly sensitive. Their whole bodies are very complex receptors that can tell them the smallest things about their world. Imagine seeing the universe through the eyes of the plants. What do you see/ feel?

Practice seeing the world for a while through the eyes of plants. You may begin to understand by your empathic view why it's a little limp or why it's turning a little yellow. The plant may show you space or the world that it sees, allowing you to see this environment in a completely different way.

This type of exercise is the foundation of all empathy. You don't have crops to deal with. Anything that animates or does not animate the weather will work. It is pure selfish garbage that makes you believe that a chair or a pencil does not share the personal reality. All of the things you can tap into are rich in information and experience.

When you develop and progress in your compassion, you start to see more depth of detail. You will have access to more information and better understand some of the information's subtleties. Eventually, you might do this exercise with someone else. Your lover or best friend, maybe. Your intuitive interaction with one another will blow your mind!

The Aware Empath Color Chameleon

Feeling the energy and seeing how empathic the aura perceives an aura is a colored light, emanating from everything and formed by energetic vibrations. It can be seen in human beings, animals, plants and, and even inanimate objects. It is surrounded by layers and shaped like an egg. The aura will give you information about your energy, emotions, and health. They are most often seen around people's heads, shoulders, and pets and a few inches in length. Auras of living things regularly change according to inner and external stimuli, well-being, and emotions in a state of flow and motion.

Empaths are highly sensitive individuals who feel and connect to another human, site, and animal energies. Developed empathy can tune into everything and feel the energy. Consider that all is energy, and the difference between the two is simply the frequency, the speed it vibrates.

Yoda was right, energy is all over, and everything flows, and empathy will train into perception, perceive and communicate with it. Empaths sense power, link to it and obtain any information they hold. Nevertheless, empathy can only translate this knowledge according to its development level, just as a computer can only use its operating software to calculate. If the software is Windows 5.1 and Windows 8.1 is necessary for information, it will not be interpreted. Empathy has a level of development and strengths and weaknesses (along with the personality). Maybe your level of development is very high. Will you view energy as an aura? The strength might not necessarily be in the clarity (explicit knowledge) or auditory realm (clairaudience). Each empath is a unique person who expresses his gifts differently. Could you practice to improve your vision and learn to see the aura? There is a practice: put the person before a white background very softly illuminated.

A background color affects the aura colors, so you have to start with white. Pick one place to look at. The center of the front is right. This is a position of the so-called brow or 3rd eye. See this position for 30 to 60 seconds or longer. After 30 seconds, analyze your peripheral vision and still look at the same location. It is essential to continue the concentration. Resist the temptation of looking around. You will note that the area near the person is darker and has a different color from the background. That's your aware of the aura. The longer you stare, the more you see it. It takes patience and practice to achieve it. Try it!

Seven auric bodies are present. The human body which involves emotions of the heart, physical comfort, enjoyment, and safety. The etheric body that comprises thoughts and feeling. Self-acceptance and self-love components are found here. The vital body that is about the rational mind is having a linear, clear, balanced view of circumstances. The astral body, as you refer to others. The bottom psychological body is spiritual in you. Alignment with the divine within allows you to commit yourself to speak and to follow the truth. The higher mental body puts you together with divine love and spiritual fulfillment — finally, the divine mind's spiritual body and the openness to serenity. The relation to God's consciousness also allows you to grasp the broader trends, a universal perspective.
This is an eagle view versus a mouse view (only when you see what's right in front of you).

The colors and interpretations of the auras will help you determine your own and other peoples' energy well-being. Red is intense, sexual, energetic, and passionate about the root chakra. It can reflect your healthy ego if it is bright and clear. It reflects a grounded state based on what is right and reliable if it is deep Red. A muddied red, however, refers to anger and is considered harmful. A bright and light rose color refers to loving tenderness and can reflect a sensitive and affectionate disposition. It is deep red, but it shows immaturity. Red-orange is a brave, competent, and innovative force. Orange represents emotions (second chakra), vitality, and good health in general. Yellow-orange suggests creative intelligence.

Yellow is the solar plexus chakra in the aura and is the energy of life force. It is the color of understanding, manifestation, and optimism. Light or pale yellow expresses evolving mental and spiritual consciousness and development.

Green refers to the chakra of the chest. A healthy natural color. This shows growth and balance in the aura. It reflects the love between human beings, animals, and nature. This is an aura of a healer, social person, or teacher. Yellow-green indicates a creative spirit and a power for interaction. It can represent the negative energy of jealousy and resentment if dark or muddy forest green.

In the auric field, blue refers to the chakra of the throat. A beautiful bright blue or turquoise light shows clear communication, possible farsightedness. Whether it is dark or dull blue, it expresses fear, self-expression, or fear of confronting or telling the truth. Indigo is the third chakra's color and reflects intense sensitivity and intuition. Violet relates to the chakra, although some also have a bright white light. It is associated with self-adjustment but also with the higher self, the spiritual. It is your divine visionary, idealistic, and artistic expression.

Chapter 15

Empathic Children

Empathy makes other people important to us and teaches us that we understand and express our emotions with the people around us. Empathy exists in early bonding between mother and child. Even before birth, a womb baby is receptive to the mother's feelings, whether positive, neutral, or negative.

When born, a baby shows tolerance to the anger, stress, and anxiety of both parents and their affection, care, and reactivity. You probably saw how they imitate your facial expressions with a smile. You can also weep if you hear another baby cry. This kind of response is a step in building empathy and sharing other people's feelings.

Babies absorb people's mental and emotional energies. They filter nothing; they receive nothing. This empathic ability will increase as a child grows old and gets out of control.

Some children get the emotions, energy, or thoughts of others to the extent to which their social and emotional lives are overwhelming and interrupted.

Because these children don't know how to set personal limits (or how to do so), they can't understand how invasive that person can be when they're in a person's mental or emotional space. It can also reduce the vibrational frequency of the infant.

Empathy is sensitive to visible and invisible things like the feelings, emotions, and diseases around it. Empathy can get hunches, see mental photos, hear voices, or have an intestine that gives people and situations hidden information. They may also feel physically in their bodies, allowing them to know where someone is afflicted.

You may have heard of Indigo kids or Crystal kids who have remarkably intuitive talents and incredible adults.

These empathetic kids easily capture adults' and other feelings and thoughts and unconsciously reach into the fields of human and spiritual energy for information and understanding.

When you look at your spiritual eyes, feel your spiritual senses, hear your spiritual ears, tell about past lives or things, see ghosts, or know something of a person or situation you do not have anybody else. Today, as many as one children in four have this ability and are always tuned to the higher frequency.

For an adult, being an empath is very exhausting. Imagine how it feels to be an intuitive or empathetic child and how it does not speak the language to your parents or teachers. A child overloaded with others' energy may have the ongoing disease, depressive episodes, anger, cry unreasonably, or "fix" things between adults who argue or do not get along well. A child or a teenager who sees or listens in the spiritual realm can act because they are overwhelmed and cannot express what they experience. The problem is compounded when adults do not listen to the child, try to hush it, or refuse to believe the child reports mental incidents.
If we invalidate their perceptions and intuitive skills, we do our intuitive kids a significant injustice. However, many parents don't know what to do with children who see or hear spirits, talk about the deceased relatives they have never met in their

bodies, give hints about past lives, forecast future events, or know a particular family secret they haven't had to deal with.

In some cases, the "Hushing" parent also has supernatural powers that he or she cannot speak openly about. Maybe it was surprised by its parents and merely imitated their parental role model. As parents, counselors, and teachers, children must be instructed how to use this empathic gift correctly, but many adults do not trust their intuition, much less recognizing their children's spiritual abilities. Empathetic children need someone to talk to and need the information to keep their auras clear, open and shut intuitive skills at will, and set energetic limits. But where do adults know how to support such empathetic children and adolescents?

Do some people's children have empathy?

Although all people have a physical body, it doesn't mean they live in the same way. When you think about why it's so, you might reflect on how we are born and how these conditions can be the defining factor.

However, without even moving to the factors that could explain why people see life differently, there are also differences in what is happening in someone. It doesn't just say that you have a physical body with the same level of empathy as somebody else.

Some individuals can be identified as a combination of empathy, and then others are out of control. One could be in a position to have no understanding or too much empathy.

Non-existing

If you have no compassion, it's not only a risk to yourself, and it's also dangerous for the people around you. And they might even be marked as a psychopath. There's a possibility that someone like this can be in prison but can also be found in the business world.

One's lack of empathy can then be what led them to finish behind bars while at the same time, enabling them to rise to the top of their profession. No compassion will not assist you in relationships but will help you in certain areas of life.

More than Enough

If you are too empathetic, you are unlikely to be a danger to others, but it might be a danger to yourself. And although they may not be called cold, they may be labeled as overly sensitive.

You could do your best to avoid situations where too much is going on, and you could spend too much time on your own. You're not then in a room by force alone, and you are there by choice.

This may mean that you can form deeper links with others and warm people to them, but it may also prevent one from doing so. It could be overwhelming to be around others, which might mean that one can not use its enhanced feeling to improve one's life.

If you have compassion, it will be another part of who you are and not something that will need to dictate your life. Out of reach, If you have an increased sense of empathy, it won't be another part of your life. It may finally define your life.

One will not feel like another part of them is their empathy; one will feel that their empathy is in control. Then no one can decide whom they empathize with or protect their soul because they will have no choice.

It doesn't matter whether you talk to something or are in a social environment and just go through someone as you're going to do it in the same way. It will suffice to be around other people to know what they feel. Being around others will bomb you and make you feel defenseless.

It doesn't matter whether you care for or don't care (or even face them) because you still consume what you do. One is like a sponge in the sea. In the beginning, water will be on its side, and the whole sponge will be submerged as time passes.

When you're around people, you will struggle to preserve your sense of yourself. And this is because they embody what happens around them, and what happens is probably a mystery for them.

Yes, you can find it difficult to distinguish between your feelings and others ' feelings. Who they are will depend on who they are with because there are no frontiers.

While there is a chance that you have started experiencing life as an adult, you have likely experienced it for the majority of your life. And when you live this way, you are often described as empathy.

It was said that people were born in this way and that their genetics are involved. Many people think people were like this because of what happened in their infancy.

A Closer Look

If you are looking at the way empathy lives, you may conclude that it is not a particular capability due to children's trauma. If you think that your life is under threat, your focus is no longer divided into what happens inside you and what is happening without you; it will take place around you.

And if a child feels threatened, he or she will probably have less control than if he were an adult. It might not be secure for them to have borders and thus protect themselves.

What can be safe is that they stay unbounded and allow the people around them to do whatever they want.

Survival Mode

It would not have been safe for them during the early years; they would have had to survive. The way the people around them felt was not something they had just to gain' approval'; it had to be done to either avoid being hurt or to know when they would be destroyed.

By living in such a place where people were focused on others, and the people around them only concentrate on their own needs, one could not have realized that they were separated and impaired their development. They would, therefore, have ignored their needs and feelings and could not establish boundaries.

Consciousness

The years are gone, but their sense of self has not grown, and one is still in a symbiotic state.

They will need to process what happened to them all these years, and as this happens, they will start to grow a sense of themselves, and their limits will also start to grow.

This doesn't mean that you won't get this ability anymore, but it probably means you're starting to settle down and understand yourself. You can then use this ability to improve your life instead of something that makes your life miserable.

Emotional volatility: Trapped Emotional instability?

Although emotional stability is the ideal, not everyone can relate to it. However, this does not mean that people who experience emotional stability are often stable and live without damage.

To be a human being is that we are emotional beings, and thus unless you become emotionally numb and disconnected, you will experience ups and downs emotionally. This is part of life and not something that should be dismissed.

If you are in contact with both sides of your emotional spectrum, you can feel good and not so good. You may feel down or weak because you have experienced some sort of loss.

And loss, either by the loss of a person or a particular position, will lead to emotional instability.

There will be some ideas about how long the pain lasts, but people will respond differently, so the pain is not stoned.

There are five stages of grief, but how long these stages last will vary from person to person. Nor is it always a linear process.

Stability

So, if you encounter emotional instability in times of failure and a moderate feeling of uncertainty elsewhere, you will be seen as reasonably balanced individuals. They are together emotionally and will not suffer from instability emotionally as a way of life.

Their conduct is entirely consistent, simply because they usually feel the same inside. What they dress could also represent the internal peace and prevent them from looking uncontrolled.

Your ability to plan and coordinate will also be active. To do this, you must be able to think clearly, and when your feelings are balanced, this will, of course, be much simpler.

These people could be assumed to have less stress than others and therefore are calmer.

There might be a piece of truth, but they are more strong and significant. Challenges can occur, and yet they can deal with storms and not cause them to be affected. So things are generally kept in proportion instead of building a mountain out of a molehill.

Balance

This allows you to experience a sense of balance and work together with your mind and emotions. And if you have always lived life in this way, it will be difficult for you to understand how it should be for someone who does not live in the same fashion.

To people who know only how emotionally unstable it feels, the above sound like a dream. They could conclude that life is always the way for them.

Instability

This determines their entire life for some people, and it may just surface in certain circumstances for others. No matter when, where, or how much it happens, it will build somebody's challenges.

It will be a problem to be able to have a sense of inner balance and harmony. Mood swings are something they know, and their behavior will reflect this. You can feel good about yourself for a moment. The next minute you are down, and you can't stand being in your own business.

From time to time, this can happen, or it can happen regularly for them. It ensures that their ability to prepare and arrange things will also be affected. Erratic and impulsive actions could be the norm, leading to a host of problems.

Consequences for some individuals, this can lead to expenses or nutrition. They might be friendly one minute and unpleasant and even aggressive the next. Plans could be made and last minute canceled.

Emotionally, one may have gotten used to feeling depressed and then know that they will be alive and willing to take on the world soon. The dress style of this individual can fluctuate to reflect its internal instability. These are examples, and there will be more.

What's the matter?

If you are that way, you might end up being labeled as having some sort of disorder. This can then lead to a particular identity and a limited personality or a bipolar nature.

Some people say it's because of genetics, while others say it's because of what happened during their infancy. Perhaps in both views, there is some reality. What is clear, though, is that when someone becomes emotionally unstable, they have no way to regulate their emotions.

Emotional regulation

This does not exist for them, which means their emotions are totally out of control.

It is a little like how a traffic light makes it possible to control the traffic and not come all at once. Without the lights, all traffic would go at once, and nothing more than accidents and collisions would occur.

The lights regulate the traffic, and, in the case of a human, it prevents one from being overwhelmed by their emotions. Since this ability is so important, it can seem odd not to have it.

Childhood

It's vital to have an empathic and conscious caregiver, but this doesn't always happen. And if it's missing, it can make you grow without the ability to regulate yourself.

Thus, as a baby and a young child, you cannot regulate how you feel. This means that they rely entirely on their caregivers and the people around them to control their feelings.

Now, if you are a caregiver who is empathetic and mostly accessible, you're probably fine. By being guided by your caregiver, you will soon internalize this capacity and develop your brain in the right way.

But if they are not fully present, or more or less completely absent, this skill will not grow, and you are left to deal with your emotions. They won't just learn this capacity, and they also have to isolate themselves from their feelings to escape emotional pain and survive.

These emotions will be trapped in their bodies and thus have to deal with today's feelings and the emotional development of the past.

It's not going to be like a raindrop, like a tidal wave. And as they've been building up for that long, it won't be amazed that someone has so many ups and downs. Rainfall will not do much, but it would cause far more damage if these rainfalls were built up over many years. And the same goes for emotions that create consciousness.

There will be two issues here. First of all, you must release your pinned emotions from your emotional body, and secondly, you must develop the ability to control yourself. Both can be achieved with the assistance of a counselor or a healer.

Here you can get in contact with your feelings and release them slowly. And through the therapists or the healers, which are mirrored and tuned, one can gradually internalize what is taking place and develop, thereby regulating oneself. Everybody is different, so the time it takes varies naturally from person to person.

The mental guide

A psychic can feel others' emotions and feelings (also known as an "empath").

Nonetheless, it is sometimes hard to tell the difference between an empathic psychic and a sensitive person. Here are some questions when you ask yourself if you have any empathy:

• Was I more sensitive to emotions than others?

The empathy of emotions and feelings appears to be extremely sensitive. This goes far beyond what non-psychics consider a "normal" impression. Sometimes, things such as the sight of a dead bird or a flower's wilting make the emotional response empathic.

• Do I get emotional for no apparent reason?

When a person experiences others' emotions, particularly if he is not close, it can seem as if empathy is in no way emotionally rolling. For example, when you go down the street, you can feel the emotions of someone you don't know a few blocks away. You cannot even see the guy, so your emotional response may seem to have come from nowhere.

• May I know how other people feel, even if they hide the truth from everyone else?

Empathy is not fooled when people face a brave face for the rest of the world in an emotional challenge.

If most people who are "normal" don't notice or realize anything was wrong, a sense of empathy is painfully aware of the truth. Empaths can see people placing themselves on a brave face. Their emotional intelligence is far superior to that of others.

Empaths -Who are you going to in times of necessity?

Empathy can easily be affected by other people's feelings. It's a career threat when you can hear what other people feel. Even if you know how to administer your empathy, there are times when you are affected by those around you, especially in times of need where you are most likely to absorb somebody else's feelings unconsciously.

It raises an important question for Empaths: with who will you spend time feeling unhappy?

When you have problems at work, you are more likely to decide to talk about them with someone.

Also unhappy because you are going to add their unhappy feelings to your miserable feeling! Soon you will feel like a pressure cooker ready to explode! What a snowball effect.

If you have lunch instead of happy at work, you "dress up" by bringing in their feelings of satisfaction. As Empaths, you do not have to speak to them because you can feel their emotions directly. It will uplift you to be in their presence and let them surround you with positive emotions.

Conversely, if you feel secure, you can choose to elevate others by transmitting your feelings of happiness around them!

Remember that everyone has the necessary biological equipment to read the emotions of others. Empathy becomes more sensitive to emotions and, hopefully, more conscious of understanding others.

This is also a significant reason why Empaths spend a lot of time alone. You don't usually like crowds or parties.

Generally, you prefer one chat, where it's much easier to track who feels what. Sadly, so many Empathies believe that they do this because something is wrong. That they should be in large groups of people there. They have got "issues" and can't lead a healthy life. This is not real! This is not true!

A great idea is spending time alone when you feel vulnerable! It simplifies things so much that you can focus on how you feel instead of figuring out yours and what's theirs. Often it's the most amusing thing you can do.

Please don't beat yourself as a personal favor because you spend a lot of time alone. That doesn't mean that you have been broken. You can't make friends, that doesn't mean. This means that you are intelligent enough to know what you need.

Chapter 16

Infection Emotional Being an "Emotional Sponge"

Empathy is a universal ability for human beings.

They define it as a severe psychological disorder if it is absent or insufficient, for example, in autism or psychopathy cases.

However, like most other human qualities, empathy in some people may be innately stronger. It can also be encouraged or defended consciously or unconsciously. Some people are, therefore, highly and almost excessively empathetic to others. Sometimes, they describe themselves as "emotional sponges," absorbing those good and bad feelings around them.

The earliest form of communication is empathy.

Human beings interact from birth with empathy. Mothers and children read each other's emotional messages correctly. That awareness is never lost, and we all use empathetic consideration of other people's emotions to support and illuminate what they say. We are all aware that the same words in a sensitive or cynical voice can have very different effects and emotional consequences.

However, we seldom think of this subliminal communication and usually don't know how we do it.

Anxiety and anger are the most' catching' feelings. While all emotions can be transmitted empathically among people, stress and color are the most problematic.

There are good reasons for this development.

Every higher animal is prone to environmental risk signals from others around it. An alarm signal prepares you for self-protection, whether it is fighting or flying. Action preparation requires neural, muscular, and endocrine responses that we perceive as physical expressions of fear and stress.

Interpersonal interpretation of Signal-Visual and auditory shifts reflect anxiety.

Psychological scientists have noted that harmful signs can be evident in humans: sweating, breathing shallow, tense postures, blushing, general restlessness.

There are also audible indications: voices can become loud or shrill, voice pitch can rise, or AR rhythmically switch between high and low, speeds can rush or talk, pause shortage, interruption of others, changes of speech velocity, or inadequate laughing. The reverse photo also shows anxiety: long pauses, faltering language, and the introduction of non-words such as "uh" or "ah."

Semantic or textual observations.

Anxiety can be indicated by an increase in the number of words related to thoughts, personal pronouns, and subjective qualifications, which the reader recognizes as reflecting self-concern when distressed conversations are transcribed. Expressions of self-instigated acts suggest anger, 'doing' instead of 'feeling.' By contrast, a relaxed attitude is distinguished by an increase in the number of substantive nouns and objective qualifications.

All this and more details are absorbed unconsciously or semi-consciously by an interlocutor or bystander and intuitively understood as signals of alarm or excitement, which can trigger anxiety or emotion in them.

Human beings tend to imitate and synchronize the facial expressions of others' facials, vocalizations, positions, and motions and, therefore, converge emotionally.

Mirror neurons are next to the motor neurons that send signals of movement to our muscles. Mirror neurons, however, fire when we observe gestures, especially deliberate gestures in others. We experience the gestures ourselves microscopically inwardly when we watch another person do something. Most of the time, this is not translated into practice. Still, most of us are familiar with the movements of a skater or a skier on Television, or "bouncing in our seats," encouraging a favorite competitor to speed up a race. These are forms we prove that we believe empathically in other people's efforts.

However, participation in the experience of others is not restricted to copying gestures.

In the sense of physical and verbal changes in others, which have to do with feeling, there are many "gestures." These indications are also reacted by our mirror neurons and are now the basis for empathy. Sadly, it is the source of psychological disease and contributes to circumstances in which people can "capture" their environments' emotions unintentionally and unwillingly.

Reducing this tension, good and bad, when the anxiety and emotional contagion are mild, small reactions like nervous laughing may shake it off or relieve it.

If it is stronger, an individual can intuitively try to cope with this interpersonal pressure by attempting to calm or reassure the others to stop sending anxiety or wrath. This is how a good parent could behave if a child communicates its distress.

However, when the other person's emotional pressure is not quickly relieved, a sensitive person can be drawn into an ongoing cycle of care and comfort that can be exploited or abused.

An example of this could be a sibling who calls and releases all her anxiety and tension late at night into her sister. The caller leaves the exchange feeling temporarily relieved and soothed, and the caller has now been thrown and worried all night. Continued emotional contagious experience is "pernicious" and can cause harm over time.

One of the peculiarities that the sender often tries to get rid of or "evacuate" feelings is that they don't like to feel or think about themselves or others. As a result, they are oddly reluctant to understand the opinions of the recipient. We sometimes deny their fear or anger and can assault their partner by showing signs of this vulnerability as we respond with empathic contagion.

This leaves the recipient in a psychologically tricky position to assume that he is the only one to feel anxious or angered or upset.

As a result of the other's negation, feelings evoked by emotional contagion are often not known to occur in the other, and the recipient may try to explain these strange, unpleasant feelings as though they were their own.

It leads to internal interactions where a sensitive, reactive person will criticize himself for "no cause" and concern for his or her mental health or wellbeing.

The recipient can look for stress relief in unhealthy ways, such as beverage, over-food, smoking, video spiel, shopping, or other distractions, left with the burden of unpleasant sensations.

Emotional contagion finds its way into the "We are all more just human than we are otherwise" recipient because all human beings, under certain circumstances, are vulnerable to feelings of anxiety, rage, fear, and hopelessness. Emotional contagion rings our social clots and makes us look for reasons for our unpleasant feelings within ourselves.

Emotional contagion recipients can sometimes even unconsciously create problems because they may find situations that justify their unexplainable anxiety, hopelessness, depression, or desperation.

Sensitivity helps.

Being mindful that you can sympathize with another person's emotions can go a long way to avoiding the worst outcomes. It can encourage the fragile individual to say, "Is this more in line with my partner than myself at this time?"

Recognizing that feelings are infectious will indicate how your contagion behaviors can be controlled. It may sometimes be emotionally wise to limit the time you spend with depressed, bitter, or angry people in a psychological environment.

Concerning emotional reactions, the focus on oneself only or the other can be equally blinding in social interaction. The most critical information can be acquired by alternating one's reactions and observing one's partners and then moving to another analysis level to focus on what is happening. Speaking with a trusted friend, counselor, or therapist can help get your perspective back on the situation and stop the troubling inner discussions about helplessness or inferiority.

Short-run emotional contagion is a correct and valid form of interpersonal communication.

A sensitive and aware person can use it to empathically understand another person's real feelings and do everything necessary to reduce others' tension. But it's time to learn more about it when it begins to attack your long-term mental and emotional balance.

Empathy binds us to the souls of others. Where does our empathy go?

Empathy is the capability to put one in the shoes of another emotionally, the ability to share and understand another person's emotions, perspectives, and feelings, both positive and negative. Empathy is the relationship and personality that binds us as individuals.

We show empathy in statements such as, "I can see that you are uncomfortable," and, "I can understand why you would be upset." We show empathy by hugging, tranquilizing touches, and even a "high five" when our empathy is about success.
Empathy is not the same emotion as friendship. Where insight allows us to experience and identify with others' feelings, sympathy is a sense of pity or sorrow for others' opinions. We feel empathy with another person, sympathy with another person.

There are many hypotheses about nature and the nutritional dimension of empathic development. Are some born good and some born evil?

For several years, stress causes the brain to release oxytocin as people feel for other people. Similarly, a study concluded that human empathy was associated with a particular variant of the oxytocin receptor gene. The study found that those with this gene variant have a more empathetic personality. Research shows that some people, approximately five percent of our population, may have a gene variant, making them less empathic. In other words, some people are more or less oxytocin-immune.

There is, therefore, scientific evidence that the character of goodness is coded in our genes. Yet nurture is not the only factor that influences it. We may be born to empathy, but our ability to apply, care for, and understand is learned conduct.

Social psychologists believe empathic behavior is focused on babies firmly attached to their family or primary carers. Empathy with them and others are influenced by their environment, in children whose parents continuously show, teach, and strengthen sincere empathy. It is a gradual emergence of the consistency and cares they receive in their formative years of social and emotional development. In many cases, but not all, adults without empathy were abused or neglected during their childhood.

Those with extremely painful children, sexually, emotionally, or physically abused children often lose touch with their feelings while shutting off from pain.

We are saddled with difficulty, be it their own or others, by their undeveloped coping skills and their lack of capacity to witness their pain. As adults, their intricate defensive mechanisms block guilt and shame and prevent their consciousness. They live by threats, fear, isolation, and punishment instead of kindness and compassion.

The opposite is exact in some situations: the person over-identifies with others' suffering, becomes overwhelmed by it and becomes too empathic to absorb all people's feelings around him. When they see others suffering and in pain, their internal pain is caused, and thus, they are worried about the pain of all and make it theirs.

A new study by the University of Michigan at an annual meeting of the Psychological Sciences Association claims that college students who began school after 2000 have empathy levels 40% lower than their 30 years before. The sharpest drop in the last nine years has occurred. The study contains data from more than 14,000 students.

One reason for this is that students become more self-oriented as their environment becomes more competitive. Some people say social networking creates a more selfish generation. Leading researchers say that today's college students are harder to sympathize with others because many of their social interactions are performed via a computer or cellular phone rather than through real-life experiences. They can choose with their friends online to whom they will react and whom they will adapt. This is more likely to lead to real life.

This is also an up-and-coming generation of video games. Data from computer-generated images and violent cyber encounters have affected many of their formative years of development. There must be a reference. This can partly explain its generation's numbness.

A movement, therefore, started to build a community that celebrated self-expression, self-love, and self-esteem. This is all good and good, or so it seems, but more narcissism was generated by the emphasis unintentionally.

All this has resulted in background aggression, lack of care for others, materialism, and shallow values.

Surely many of us do not speak for society as a whole in this way.

We live today under relentless internal and external life pressures. Our nation is facing economic crises, violence, conflict, crime, massive job insecurity, and political corruption daily. Wherever we look, we see the disintegration of ethics.

Where did we appreciate quality literature as a society?

And what happened to our system of law? It has been shown repeatedly that the innocent's rights take their seats behind the offender's rights. Our laws control criminals very little. It seems that criminals control the law. If a disorder of empathy could ever spur unthinkable violence in an ordinary person, it is time.

Scientists have studied empathy from various approaches, together with physiological and psychological roots. Since people are made up of mind, body, and soul, that is perfectly reasonable. Several things affect our actions.

The intangible concept of evil examines a theory that there are empathy levels and lie within a more explanatory spectrum.

The empathy level of a person comes from a lower brain empathy circuit. The function of this circuit determines the location of a person within the range of empathy. The degree of understanding of a person, six degrees are high functioning empathy circuits, and zero is a low functioning circuit.

Classifies as zero-negative those with narcissistic personality disorders and psychopathic, people without the ability to feel other people's feelings and not self-regulate others' treatment.

The better and perhaps most popular way of assessing empathy is through a questionnaire called the "Interpersonal Reactivity Index," which defines empathy as "the reactions of one person to the experiences of the other person." The survey uses 5-point scales (A= does not describe me well in

E= very good in describing me). This scale is used to calculate a person's perspective.

Because empathy starts with knowledge of other people's feelings and receptiveness to subtle signals in women's skills, females typically gain more in these kinds of tests.

Those who have felt an enormous variety of emotions and those who think the most can also identify more with others. Typically, these people are not a threat to society. But some are empathic. These are the people who pose risks to our community. These are time bombs that can explode at any moment.

Conclusion

An empath enables us to see the user from more points of view. Patterns state a lot, as well as contradictions-- which is essential information. It can occur that a user is not happy about the service but still utilizes it. Alternatively, they have a very positive feeling about service, however not using it as frequently. These are concerns that require to be researched even more.

Although it is a beneficial tool to visually introduce a user, it ought to be taken into account that an empathy map reveals a state at a specific moment in time. For that reason, it is worth returning to your plan from time to time and keep including presumptions and insights, particularly after talking or observing with consumers similar to your profile.

We are all capable of feeling emotions in others. It is a simple survival ability for humans and animals. This ability typically diminishes in infancy as we begin to rely on verbal rather than emotional signals.

On the other hand, empathies have increased the reaction to other people's feelings, which continue to develop over time. As other children stop emotional evidence, they are entirely overwhelmed by the small amount of emotional information received in social environments.

Decision fatigue refers to the decline in the quality of individual decision-making after a lengthy decision-making session.

This concept has been thoroughly studied in psychology, where people who have to make many decisions within their daily work, such as judges, are worn out over time and tend, later on, to make more unfortunate decisions.

The mind is exhausted, and it is challenging to assess trade-offs, a critical decision-making skill. Likewise, the constant emotional information they have to process will excessively trigger empathy.

This is especially true for damaged empaths who have difficulty regulating the flow of emotions from others. Over time, their ability to respond to emotions appropriately may be unpredictable, leaving them weak and depressed.

Under an Empath Blues spell, without knowing why, you might start feeling sad. You are also more likely to feel down later in the day, wake up well in the morning, then have a decreased positive feeling as the day passes.

Empath blues are usually temporary; if left unattended, it can become chronic. So what can you do if you're in the throes of the Empath blues?

A widespread misunderstanding that is trying to be "happier" is the remedy for emotional fatigue. It means that, while you feel naughty, you should try to think positively. Have you ever been to somebody who wanted to encourage you while you were sad? You want them to shut up and go, despite their best efforts.

Feeling happy is a robust emotion and strong emotions, positive or negative, which in the first place have caused emotional tiredness. Not only that, but it takes a lot of effort to cheer on the spot when you are down. When you are exhausted, you try to spring from one end of the emotional spectrum (sadness) to the opposite end (happiness), so you will most likely fall flat mid-spring on your face. Most empaths don't know the condition of emotional silence needed to deal with emotional tiredness. We are so used to being pulled in all sorts of feelings that feeling nothing is always equivalent to feeling dead or hollow.

You wonder if there's anything wrong. And yet, it's nothing other than body sleep! We need time to relax, body, mind, and emotions. Luckily, empathy is often very intuitive beings. You're attracted to what's right for you. That is why if you are an empathy, you would possibly understand some of your impulses to alleviate emotional exhaustion in the four most effective ways.

Being in nature: Many people feel most peacefully in the countryside, trees, and large water bodies like the ocean or a lake. For good reasons! Trees and water give the emotional vibration a natural "white noise." It's like wearing a noise headset that cancels out people's emotions.

Being alone: Empathies need time on their own, where others' emotions are less likely to be tuned. It doesn't mean that you're anti-social or don't like men! It only means that you have to refuel before you return to the world. Ensure that you have a lot of time alone when doing something not emotional, such as gardening, knitting, cooking, etc.

Physical exercise: Physical activity will help you cope with mental tiredness by shifting your focus away from your feelings and physical body. The physical activity must be intense enough for our purposes to warrant your full attention. Rock climbing and yoga were my favorites in emotionally calm activities.

Meditation: Meditation offers a powerful way to distract the mind from others. To empathizes who prefer to always listen with others, it can be very challenging. At first, it can feel unnatural or painful. Creating a quiet place within your mind and emotionally sensitive body by calming your breath or following a guided audio meditation can provide you with the space you need to relax. You probably struggle with a lot of aspects of daily life if you're an Empath.

One of the significant problems with empaths is that they tend to take on other people's feelings and concerns as if they were their own. When you feel other people's opinions, you often don't understand that emotions come from outside. We all tend to feel as if they are very frustrating and often distracting feelings.

You can get very sick after a while of accumulating emotions, both yours and others. Some new life skills must be developed and applied to move beyond these difficulties. There are several ways to address empathy problems. Many of them are to describe and justify who you are and what you believe. The most and first crucial stage is to reflect on your thoughts and beliefs. When you become much more transparent and aware of who you are and what you believe relative to what other people think, you will broaden the distance between yourself and others' feelings. Even if you take on others' opinions, it will be easier to recognize them as not yours. Once recognition is made, the other persons' stuff' can quickly be released.

Sharon Copeland

Want more?

Grab My Book "Back to Self-Care FOR FREE in the following page" – Limited Copies Available

This is Not The End

Hi there!

Congratulations! You just reached the end of the book!

You digested a lot of information about the topic and I really hope you discovered something new and inspiring!

You know what comes next :)

Well, beside leaving a review on the book at the link below, I share the link to the FREE BOOK so that you can keep on reading! That's why "This Is Not The End"

>>You can Leave a Review Here<<

If you have any feedback, please get in touch with me at the following contacts, I have them at the beginning of the book, but for your convenience I drop them here too!

Website: sharoncopeland.com

Email: info@sharoncopeland.com

Facebook Page: https://swiy.io/SharonCopelandFBPage

Facebook Support Book:
https://swiy.io/SharonCopelandFBGroup

Instagram: @saroncopelandauthor

Happy Reading!

SHARON COPELAND

Back to
Self-Help

Self-Healing Tips to Take Care of Your Body and Spirit.
Overcome Stress, Depression, and Panic Attacks with
Mindfulness Meditation

>> Discover the Secrets of Self-Help, IT'S FREE!<<
Or Scan This Code With your Phone Camera

www.ingramcontent.com/pod-product-compliance
Lightning Source LLC
Chambersburg PA
CBHW070150310326
41914CB00089B/772